Dedication

To Patti and Ron

Acknowledgments

No project like this would be possible were it not for the support of our families. A special thank you to Ron Collier and Patti Regehr Magid for their patience, understanding, and support. There were weeks when Anne and Larry spent more time with each other than they did with their respective spouses and families. Thanks also to Sam and Will Collier, for being good critical thinkers and safe online socialisers and for allowing "Mom" to be "author" for a while, and to Katherine Magid and Will Magid, both recent graduates of teenage-hood, for providing sage advice as social-networking experts who don't have to reach too far back to remember what it's like to be a teenager. Thanks also to our young friends Susan, Cameron, Lisa, and many anonymous teenage participants in the BlogSafety forum for serving as our native guides in the world of social networking.

We are indebted to Danah Boyd at the University of California, Berkeley, for glimpses into her pioneering research on social networking, and also to the researchers at the University of New Hampshire's Crimes Against Children Research Center, the Pew Internet & American Life Project, and the Kaiser Family Foundation. They keep all of us current on children's use of the Web and digital media.

We want to acknowledge Detective Frank Dannahey from Connecticut in the USA for sharing his wise, balanced approach to working with online kids, and Stephen Carrick-Davies of Childnet International for his support, advice, and encouragement and for helping us understand some of the international implications of social networking. Thanks also to President Ernie Allen and our many friends at the National Center for Missing & Exploited Children for their support and inspiring work. They are great champions for our children.

This book never could have happened if it weren't for the steady, eagle-eyed editorial supervision of Jill Marts Lodwig, copy editor Kathy Simpson, production editor Connie Jeung-Mills, and the tireless contributions of Mona Bueler who helped us with the hands-on sections of this book. Thanks also to Peachpit Press's Cliff Colby and Nancy Ruenzel for encouraging us to embark on this project.

While we were writing this book, we were also in the final stages of launching BlogSafety.com, a Web forum (operated by the non-profit Tech Parenting Group) where parents, young people and experts are talking with each other about the promises and challenges of social networking. Although the site, like this book, is editorially independent, it is receiving support from sponsoring companies, including MySpace, AOL, Bebo, Facebook, Friendster, Hi5, SixApart/LiveJournal, Tagged and Xanga, as well as our hosting company, LiveWorld. These companies agreed to put aside their competitive differences to support a project dedicated to making the Web safer for children and teenagers, and we appreciate their support.

Although MySpace officials didn't review our manuscript and had no editorial control or influence, we are grateful for their technical support, their insight into the inner workings of the company, and their willingness to answer questions, especially as they were changing some of MySpace's privacy policies as we were finishing the book. Special thanks to Hemanshu Nigam, chief security officer of Fox Interactive Media, and MySpace executives Shawn Gold and Sarah Kaleel for their advice and technical assistance.

Thanks also to Bill Thompson for his work on this version of the book written for UK MySpace users. Bill appears regularly on BBC Radio and Television talking about technology, and has a weekly column on the BBC news website.

Contents

Acknowledgments	vi
Introduction	xi

CHAPTER 1
Online Socialising Basics — **1**

What *Is* Social Networking?	2
Creative Networking	3
A Parents'-Eye View	7
Teenagers Are Figuring It Out	7
Multiplying Like Rabbits	9
Not Their Parents' Web	12

CHAPTER 2
The Scene — **13**

Creating a Self, Online	14
How Public Is It?	16
Many Little Worlds	20
Acting Up in Public	22
Are They Overexposed?	24

CHAPTER 3
MySpace for Parents — **27**

Setting Up an Account	28
Personalising Your Profile	34
Adjusting Other Account Settings	48
Turning MySpace Into YourSpace	53
Calendars	60
Cancelling an Account	61

CHAPTER 4
Managing the Social Stuff — **65**

Making and Managing Friends	66
Using MySpace Mail	71

Using the Address Book   74

Using Bulletins   75

Modifying Your Top 8   76

Deleting Friends   78

Commenting on Other People's Profiles   78

MySpace Events   83

Photo Rankings   84

MySpace Communities   86

Instant Messaging   100

Blogging   102

Tackling Safety Issues   105

CHAPTER 5
Social Networking Safely   **107**

First, the Research   108

Assessing the Risks   114

What's a Parent to Do?   130

CHAPTER 6
A Parents' Toolkit   **131**

Children Want Parental Input   132

Privacy Options for Older Children   135

Reporting Misconduct on MySpace   135

Finding Your Child Online   139

Monitoring and Filtering   143

Cancelling Your Child's Account   147

CHAPTER 7
MySpacers' Advanced Tricks and Tips   **151**

Pimping and Hacking: Oh My!   152

HTML Is Key   152

Before You Customise   153

Making Profiles Sing and Dance   156

Changing Top 8 Friends to Top 20   160

Monitoring Visitors to Your Profile   161

Bots: Making Friends by the Thousands   162

Uploading Video   164

Forums for Learning About Customising   167

CHAPTER 8

Where Do We Go From Here?   **171**

Teenagers Are in the Driver's Seat   172

Parents in the Car   173

There Ought to Be a Law. . .   174

Susan's Story   175

Index   179

Introduction

If you have heard your child speak about websites like MySpace, Bebo and LunarStorm, then welcome to the new phenomenon of "social networking". Social networking has certainly arrived on the scene in the UK, having first taken off in the US. The growth of the social networking phenomenon has been astronomical, and such is the uptake that it is reported that around the world a new blog is being created every second. Users of these sites are counted in millions, even in the UK alone. Bebo, one such social networking site that only launched last year, reports having 25 million users worldwide, 5 million of those in the UK. At the time of writing, the UK site of MySpace saw its user numbers increase in the first 6 months of 2006 by 98 per cent, to 3.5 million users, putting it in the UK's top 3.

Judging by this extraordinary growth and appeal to young people, it is perhaps no surprise that social networking sites are topping the list of most popular websites with UK children, with over 60 per cent of 13–17-year-olds in the UK having profiles on social networking sites.

So what is this online social networking, how does it work, and why is it so popular, particularly with young people? This book explores the phenomenon and provides answers to these questions, by helping parents to see inside the social networking environment. It also looks at the issues that parents need to be aware of as their children engage with it, and offers advice on how to help keep the experience constructive.

Social networking can come in a variety of shapes and sizes, but the essence of it is to allow the user to create a space online in which they can present themselves and their interests in a highly visual and multimedia fashion, and to develop and maintain a network of friends and contacts around them. Websites such as MySpace and Bebo are particularly appealing to young people because they make it extremely easy for the user to create a professional-looking online presence and to develop a network of friends to interact with it.

As young people see it, it is the ability to hang out with friends online that makes these sites so great. They can personalise their own spaces with music, photos, videos, and graphics. They can explore their interests, express their tastes, feelings and opinions with all these media—among friends or to the whole world. It's like reality TV on the Web that anyone can produce. It gives them a powerful voice to express their identity and opinions and—for the most part—they are using it to good effect. For example, some musicians or bands have launched themselves entirely on the strength of this new 'stage'. And all this is for free with just one password. Is it any wonder that young people love it? Surfing and sending emails looks pretty dull by comparison.

But is this environment safe for young people? This is perhaps the most pressing and worrying question for parents. Social networking has attracted the attention of the UK national media, and if you listened to some of the newspaper headlines you would probably think not. Headlines such as 'Paedophile warning over teen websites Bebo and MySpace' (*Daily Mail*, 3rd July 2006) illustrate very clearly the widely publicised risks of children sharing their personal information and images online where anyone can see them. The risks conveyed are real, and there have been cases in the US where children have been abused by paedophiles who were able to find out about them and contact them via their social networking pages or profiles.

There is also the risk, and this is a much more commonplace one, of cyberbullying, with young people getting into harassing or malicious activity online, using social networks online to bully and victimise others, as they have with mobiles. There are clearly risks with children creating or posting inappropriate, offensive or even illegal content in their spaces. This could get them into trouble with school, friends, and even the police depending on the nature of such material. There is also the risk of children posting abusive comments on other people's spaces, or coming across potentially harmful content while looking at other people's profiles.

Following concerns about what information children were sharing, but also in response to the use of social networking as a form of cyber-bullying, we have seen some schools in the UK take the step of banning access to such sites from school computers. Social networking has also reached the attention of government and law enforcement, with the

Home Office Task Force on Child Protection on the Internet looking at this new development, as well as the new Child Exploitation Online Protection Centre, holding a series of workshops with stakeholders and young people in order to find out more about the social networking phenomenon.

This level of attention does reflect that there are real concerns. And it is important to recognise that there are potential risks. However, there remains a danger that by focusing on the risks we may forget about the benefits, and the creative way in which young people are expressing themselves and their ideas, thoughts and music online.

It is not easy talking to a young person about their social networking online or offline. So far young people have used these sites as their private domain, in much the same way as you would a personal diary and address book. However, because of the public nature of this environment and because young people have been hurt by inappropriate behaviour in these spaces, it is important that parents become involved.

One of the best ways is to ask them if they can show you their site or even add you as a contact on their buddy or friend's list. If you can't–and who would want their mum or dad lurking in the background?–at least discuss the issues with them. Being positive in such discussions will be a help. There is a lot about social networking that is good and gives young people a chance to create their own original content and stay in touch with their friends. Yes, there are dangers, but it is important not to overreact and to appreciate why these sites are appealing, and why your child may feel that they are an essential part of their social lives. Young people are not creating online profiles and blogs to scare parents, they are doing so because they need a place to gather and interact with their peers. As with most things, parents need to strike a balance between educating them to behave safely and trusting them to get on with it.

This book will equip you for that communication, and help bring you up to speed with what your children are doing online. However technology is constantly changing and we are already seeing social networking sites developing for mobile phone platforms. That's why Childnet has worked with the authors of this book and supported the development of a special www.blogsafety.com website where parents can form their own social networking and keep up to date with this phenomenon and learn the best ways to really help their children get the most out of the internet

Who knows after reading this book you may decide you too can start your own pop band on a Social Networking site, but get advice from your children first!

Stephen Carrick-Davies
CEO Childnet International

CHAPTER 1

Online Socialising Basics

WELCOME TO WEB 2.0—the everywhere, all-the-time, multi-media, multidevice, downloadable *and* uploadable, user-driven Internet. Although many of us may not be aware of all the Web's capabilities these days, rest assured that teenagers are. Not only have they figured out Web 2.0, but they're also among its most experienced producers, videographers, DJs, VJs, publishers, podcasters, and mobloggers (mobile bloggers).

Of course, teenagers aren't necessarily aware of all the Web knowledge they possess. They don't really think about whether they're creating multimedia and socialising online or offline. They just produce and socialise, using tools that happen to involve the Internet, such as instant messaging, blogs, chat, texting on phones, and social networking.

What *Is* Social Networking?

Social networking wasn't coined by teenagers; they don't use the term to describe their online activities. Young people just socialise. They update their profiles, post comments, blog, add friends (like buddies on a buddy list), and chat on what have become known by us adults as social-networking sites.

As we adults struggle to find the language that describes this phenomenon, young people are speeding ahead, making it up as they go, including the language and the tools and their uses. To them, these sites are just another tool for socialising. Sometimes, they call these sites *online communities,* but for most of them, the line between online and offline is decidedly blurred.

Trying to define social networking is very much like trying to pin down a moving target, because it's evolving so quickly. In its earliest phase, social networking was either blogging (having an online journal or being an amateur commentator) or socialising (finding friends and connecting with them).

A *blog* (short for *Web log*) is simply a Web page anyone can create without any technical know-how. Blogs were and still are easy to do because companies have created tools that are very much like word-processing applications. By simply typing words onscreen and dragging photos from their hard drives to the page, bloggers ushered in the era of desktop publishing for the Web: all of a sudden, anyone could post a Web page, and teenagers did so with a vengeance.

A parallel development was the pure social networking (more about connecting than personal punditry) that started in the '90s but really took off in 2003 with Friendster.com (**FIGURE 1.1**).

Meanwhile, blogging kept getting more interactive and adding more features, with young people fuelling this process. They have made it as much about casual communication and socialising as it is about publishing and journaling. The teenage version of blogging is now better described as social networking. Adult pundits, researchers, hobbyists, and many teenagers to this day continue to do the old kind of blogging: blogging with reader feedback (and now photos).

FIGURE 1.1 Friendster was one of the original social-networking sites.

Creative Networking

MySpace was the turning point for social networking. Unlike Friendster, which arrived on the scene at about the same time, it allowed users to combine the media-rich self-expression that blogging was beginning to offer with multiple socialising tools (IM, email, comments, buddy lists, discussion boards, and chat). Suddenly, there was something seemingly made to order for youngsters. You could call it creative networking or social producing—maybe even collective self-expression.

Friendster, to be fair, has since added a bunch of self-expression features, but it was MySpace's embrace of both publishing and socialising tools— when it mattered, when teenagers were looking for something even more social than blogs—that made it a traffic-growth record-breaker (**FIGURE 1.2**).

By mid-2005, within two years of MySpace's debut as a social-networking site, *Business Week* reported that MySpace was getting more page views than the Google search engine, and by early 2006, MySpace was welcoming around 200,000 new members a day. Overnight, it seemed, the site's population was bigger than the world's most-populated cities.

FIGURE 1.2 MySpace ushered in social producing and creative networking.

Newspapers and magazines around the world have described MySpace as a combination of an alternative-reality game, a nightclub with lots of beautiful people and wannabes, MTV, and a teenager's bedroom. According to the *Daily Mirror*, it's "the top online teenage hangout" ("MySpace bolsters protection for minors", by Kenneth Li, June 21, 2006).

In other words, teenagers took the site's name literally: it was *their* space. Grownups—especially parents—were not even on the radar screen of the average MySpace user. Despite growing evidence that parents were checking out their children's MySpace activities, young people were in denial.

Part of what made MySpace so fun for them was the very fact that parents weren't there; it was *teen* space, very much like their own rooms with the door closed or a party when parents are out of town. Yes, it was public, but "private" in a way—something like when kids go off to university. And MySpace held another contradiction that teenagers like: "safe" (anonymous) but with just enough riskiness to make it cool, and individual but also delightfully collective.

Young people today have more awareness of the public aspect of social networking, of course. But back to its appeal. . .

MySpace—in fact, the whole Web now—is basically whatever anybody wants it to be. And this is the key to understanding youngsters and Web 2.0: MySpace, social networking, and Web 2.0 in general are different experiences for everyone who uses them. Why? Because teenagers use MySpace for different things.

Profiles: The New "Chat"

Some young people spend all their MySpace time checking comments on their profiles and commenting on their friends' profiles, noting how their photos are ranked, and where they're ranked on their friends' "Top Friends" lists. In these cases, MySpace is purely social.

KEY PARENTING POINT

We parents can understand the social Web much better by talking with our own children about how they use it, rather than relying on reading news stories about it.

Designing and Decorating Spaces

Other teenagers are into visual self-expression. How you decorate your space says a lot about you. Some teenagers change background music, graphics, fonts, photos, and links often; it's a lot easier than redecorating your bedroom, and a lot more people see it.

Creating a profile is also a way to experiment with identity—something teenagers do a lot and something psychologists say they're supposed to be doing. For some MySpace users, though, profile customisation isn't just about visuals; it's also a way of showing off their technical sophistication. MySpace lets people add to their spaces software code they've written or downloaded from other sites, such as PimpMySpace.org and MySpaceCode.com. With this special code, people can add effects like glittery text, animations, clip art, and *avatars* (animated representations of themselves).

A Public Journal

For some MySpace users, the space is all about blogging or being a writer—updating their online journals every day, every week, or whenever the spirit moves them. It's like an online diary, which is a bit of an oxymoron, because this "diary" is far from private. Some users try to gain at least a little control over who reads their entries, however, by registering as 14- or 15-year-olds, in which case they have the option of letting only people on their friends lists see what they write, though MySpace now lets anyone have a private profile. Some parents and the police aren't crazy about that.

Interest Communities

MySpace has all sorts of communities.

There are very personal ones, like the people on a user's friends list, and absurdly giant personal communities, like the people on the friends list of someone who's planning to win a virtual popularity contest.

There are also macro interest communities, such as the Music, Film, Books, and Games groups. Of these, the largest by far is Music, the original MySpace community. For a lot of MySpacers, that community is what the site is all about.

Then there are groups one can join to talk about things like hobbies, sport, politics, and parenting (yes, there are parenting groups on MySpace!).

Even entire schools have created their own communities, run by a student moderator who has been designated by participants.

As with all technologies, there is an upside and a downside to online communities. Teenagers can learn a lot in groups about things like politics. The links can also be international—one 15-year-old in Cambridge has MySpace friends in Brazil with whom she discusses politics in South America. But negative or destructive interests can also be reinforced in an online community; see Chapters 5 and 6 for more on the risks of social networking and how it can be done safely.

Teenagers' blogs and social-networking spaces are just online extensions or representations of themselves and their lives, with an intriguing, unsettling dose of good ol' Internet anonymity thrown in to keep things interesting.

A Parents'-Eye View

MySpace profiles can be pretty jarring to parents when they check out the site for the first time.

The profiles may have a dishevelled look, in the way that kids and their rooms sometimes look to adults. Then there are the photos, some of which seem over the top to parents thinking about who else is viewing them. You may have seen this effect in TV news stories, in what sometimes seems like a ratings grab: the shocked looks on parents' faces when a reporter takes them to a page of search results displaying profiles of students from the school their children attend.

What parents are seeing, in effect, is what adolescents have been doing and saying for aeons in more private spaces like the local youth club, school disco, in shopping centres or at the cinema on a Friday night.

What's very different here is that all the "Ps"—peers, parents, predators, police, and policymakers—are thrown into the same space, which makes for a volatile potion! It's definitely shaking up adults.

What we need to keep in mind is that these kinds of adolescent self-expression have been going on for generations and that the content is not always "real." It's an act in a lot of cases. Remember? We experimented with who we were when we were at parties too. We're not saying everybody on MySpace is acting out, showing off, or experimenting with personas. Not even all the teenagers are, of course.

Teenagers Are Figuring It Out

OK, so experimenting with who they are is typical teenage fare.

"But it's *public*," you may say.

Exactly. That's what young social networkers have been in denial about: that we parents can actually *watch* them at this giant party.

Adults aren't the only ones who have been affected by all the media coverage of MySpace, however. Young people are becoming very aware that this isn't a truly private space where they can let their hair down away from adult scrutiny.

This growing awareness is both good and bad from a parent's perspective. The really good news is that children are getting smarter. They know that what they post on MySpace and other social-networking sites can be exploited by peers and strangers, and that they can lose control of what they upload. Comments, photos, and videos can be copied and pasted in other websites, shared on file-sharing networks, and passed around in IMs and emails.

KEY PARENTING POINT

If you suspect that your children don't know, by all means ask them if they're careful about what they say and upload on MySpace, and whether they've been harassed by peers or strangers and how they handled it.

FIGURE 1.3 Facebook started in the United States but is now also available for students at many UK universities.

The bad news about this growing awareness of adult scrutiny is that young MySpace users may just move on. Although it might seem strange to consider this bad news, keep in mind that there are zillions of other social-networking sites where kids can go (**FIGURE 1.3**). And many of these sites are less accountable, at least to shareholders. In fact, some of them, like myYearbook.com, are teeny private companies started by US high-school students during the holidays (**FIGURE 1.4**). All these options make it all the more difficult for parents to keep track of their children's online activities. And the number of these sites is only increasing.

Multiplying Like Rabbits

The sites we hear about in the news and Nielsen/NetRatings' Top 10 barely scratch the surface of community sites where children can register for free from home or anywhere there's an Internet connection.

Wikipedia, the collaborative online encyclopedia, links to nearly 5 dozen in its list of "notable social-networking sites."

FIGURE 1.4 The site myYearbook, No. 4 on the comScore Media Metrix list in December 2005, was started by American school students while on holiday.

KEY PARENTING POINT

It might be informative to check out some of these other social networks to see how people use them and then ask your children whether they use more than one. An 18-year-old American au pair in the Netherlands whom we've interviewed told us she maintains pages on MySpace, LiveJournal, and Xanga because different friends use these sites, and she wants to be able to stay in touch with all of them.

There are narrow-interest sites revolving around specific music genres; geographically-oriented sites (from small towns to whole countries); counterculture sites; teenagers-only sites; social-elite, invitation-only sites; university-oriented sites; brand-related sites hosted by marketers. . . the list goes on.

Social-networking sites are proving so popular that in July 2006 the UK's Child Exploitation and Online Protection (CEOP) Centre held a conference with young people, educators, parents and industry representatives to discuss how young people can stay safe in the new environment. In the US the FBI said in May 2006 that it had a list of around 200 social-networking sites, but this number is going to grow as users are given the tools to create their own sites just as they create their own blogs.

Social networking is also happening all over the world. Swedish, Korean, Portuguese, Chinese, Estonian, and Indian parents have a lot of the same questions and concerns we have, except that they concern Lunarstorm.se, Cyworld.com, Orkut.com, QQ.com, Connect.ee, and Hi5.com, to name just a few top sites in other countries (**FIGURES 1.5** to **1.8**).

FIGURE 1.5 More than 90 per cent of Sweden's secondary school students are members of Lunarstorm, according to the *International Herald Tribune.*

FIGURE 1.6 Orkut is a hugely popular Google site in Brazil; 11 million of its 15 million users socialise there.

FIGURE 1.7 Connect.ee is a popular social-networking site in Estonia.

FIGURE 1.8 Hi5 is a San Francisco-based social-networking site that's a favourite among young Net users in India.

Teenage social networking is, in effect, beyond control except perhaps in individual homes.

Even at home, we can say "no more MySpace," but you can see that there are burgeoning alternatives and work-arounds in and beyond the home. Laws and filters can try to block them in specific spaces, such as learning centres, schools and libraries. But with wireless broadband Internet connections now or soon available anywhere via phones, game players, video music players, PDAs, and laptops, the reach of these automated parental controls is diminishing rather than expanding.

We online-safety advocates have been saying for more than a decade that there is no substitute for engaged parenting. Well, we are saying it louder now. But that engagement, as you'll discover throughout this book, is less about control than it is about communication.

Not Their Parents' Web

We need to understand that the Web, as our teenagers use it, is not just a productivity tool or a more convenient way to find information—not even a way to share photos with distant relatives. It's not a tool as we adults see it. It's an extension of teenagers themselves.

In the US, *Fast Company* magazine recently interviewed Evan Rifkin, co-founder of TagWorld.com, a rapidly up-and-coming "social networking plus media hosting" site. Rifkin said in that interview, published in the June

2006 issue, "People want to live their lives online." This is, in fact, what's happening with our children, for whom the distinction between online and offline is blurring rapidly, as we mentioned earlier.

Because of its flexibility and all the different forms of interaction and self-expression MySpace allows, young people are able to move their lives online too. Just as water finds outlets and cracks that we never knew about, teenagers found MySpace.

CHAPTER 2

The Scene

EXACTLY WHAT ARE TEENAGERS *doing* on these sites? If you ask them, they'll most likely tell you they're "just hanging out."

Hanging out on MySpace and other social-networking sites is sort of like networking in the adult sense of the word, except that young people aren't reaching out to their extended network of friends with some purpose in mind, as we think of it. Instead, they're engaged in conveniently asynchronous but also real-time collective and interactive self-expression. Whew—it's not easy being a teenager!

Let's take a look at what this self-expression is all about, from teenagers' and the experts' points of view.

Creating a Self, Online

MySpace profiles represent teenagers' *online selves*—not so much an extension of who they are but who they see themselves to be at the moment, expressed in comments, photos, and music (**FIGURE 2.1**).

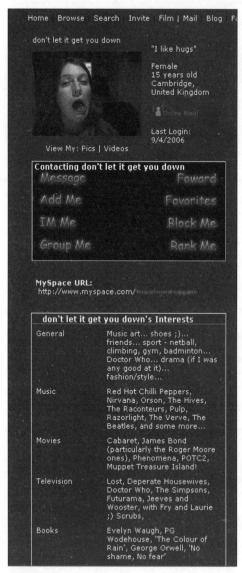

FIGURE 2.1 The MySpace profile of 15-year-old "Emma."

Part of what forms those online selves, in addition to profiles, are friends' photos and comments that appear on the same page. The combination of all these elements, which is very much a group activity, presents a self defined in relation to others (**FIGURE 2.2**).

A lot of thought often goes into these profiles, in what looks to adults like terse comments and crazy photos. This haphazardness is a natural byproduct of teenagers making up who they are as they go along. Although it may look aimless and superficial, it's actually very productive, says Danah Boyd, a pioneering social-networks researcher at the University

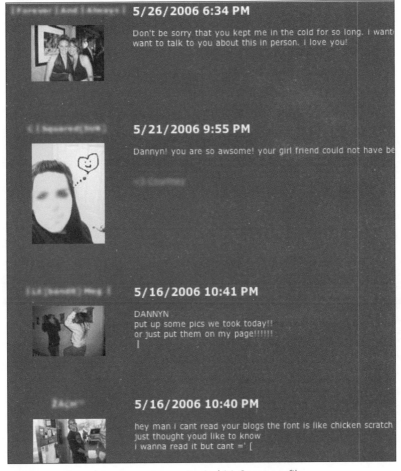

5/26/2006 6:34 PM

Don't be sorry that you kept me in the cold for so long. i want want to talk to you about this in person. i love you!

5/21/2006 9:55 PM

Dannyn! you are so awsome! your girl friend could not have be

5/16/2006 10:41 PM

DANNYN
put up some pics we took today!!
or just put them on my page!!!!!!
I

5/16/2006 10:40 PM

hey man i cant read your blogs the font is like chicken scratch
just thought youd like to know
i wanna read it but cant =' [

FIGURE 2.2 Friends' comments on a typical MySpace profile of California, Berkeley in the United States. MySpace is "not the waste of time adults think it is. What's happening in it is what academics call *informal learning*," Boyd says.

Hanging out has a lot of social value, adds Boyd. "It's where you learn social norms, rules, how to interact with others, narrative [writing a blog], personal and group history, and media literacy."

David Huffaker, a researcher of online social behaviour at Chicago's Northwestern University, agrees. "These activities are important for identity exploration, which is one of the principal tasks of adolescence," Huffaker wrote in an academic paper, "Teen Blogs Exposed: The Private Lives of Teens Made Public" which he presented at the American Association for the Advancement of Science in February 2006.

Jim Gamble, CEO of the Child Exploitation and Online Protection Centre in London, is one of the people working to make sure that the Internet is safe for children. He can see the good side of sites like MySpace as well as the risks: "social networking sites provide great opportunities for young people to meet and share experiences, but with this freedom comes a degree of risk and the need to act responsibly."

How Public Is It?

To get a sense of how differently adult visitors and younger users perceive the public aspect of MySpace, picture a mainline railway station full of people—say, King's Cross in London.

A person entering the station for the first time might take a sweeping look around, feel intimidated, and look for the nearest exit. A City commuter, on the other hand, would simply nip in and head straight for her train.

A socialising teenager entering MySpace is much like that commuter: he'll pop in and make a beeline for his friends, who are gathering in a group under the indicator board, where they *always* meet. He'll check for messages, look for the latest comments or blog postings, and type his reactions and comments.

By contrast, we parents go into MySpace very new to this phenomenon, maybe searching for a child's school or just randomly clicking profiles (**FIGURE 2.3**). Quickly overwhelmed by the vulnerability that goes with exposing oneself in such a massive public space, we might develop a sudden urge to head for the exit—and insist that our kids do the same.

FIGURE 2.3 Thousands of MySpacers' profiles are just a click away.

But children rarely use MySpace that way; they don't wander aimlessly, for the most part. When they've finished checking and updating their own profiles, they usually check their friends' profiles. "If they're really, really,

really bored, *maybe* they'll start random searching," says Danah Boyd. But young people don't search the way adults do, in a sweeping, random, out-of-the-blue fashion. They first search for people with shared interests, via their friends' profiles and friends lists, and then search their friends' friends lists and out through the concentric circles as time allows (**FIGURE 2.4**).

FIGURE 2.4 If there's searching at all, it starts with their friends list, ground zero for teen social networkers.

Purposeful, Not Random

That's how our 15-year-old friend Emma (not her real name) in Cambridge describes it. She uses MySpace to stay in touch with friends in school as well as to arrange social events like attending gigs. She also has friends from other towns, including one who is a cousin of a Brazilian schoolfriend.

Lisa, a MySpace user from California, is more focused on her profile than on joining groups or joining virtual communities. She did join one MySpace group, the online equivalent of a real-life conference that she's a member of, but this was for purely practical reasons.

"All the kids in my class involved in [the conference] couldn't always coordinate their schedules to get together at the same time. So we formed a community on MySpace to keep our meeting minutes," Lisa says. Now there's no more "You must've missed the meeting!"

Multi*socialising*

But even though all this happens on MySpace, this is not to say that social networking is happening only there. We're seeing more and more reports around the country about teen multisocialising, which is like multitasking but encompasses a whole lot more than just socialising. *Multisocialising* describes how kids simultaneously juggle devices (such as PCs, phones, game players, and MP3 players), technologies (such as IM, texting, and MySpace), people or conversations, and tasks like homework while they are socialising.

Teenagers have many layers and shades of communication styles, depending on who's involved, and what device or site is handy.

Lisa, who uses social-networking site Facebook more now that she's heading to university, says she didn't use MySpace for discussion boards or chat. Instead, she used eSPINtheBottle.com (maybe because it's for teenagers only), where she'd chat with Mike. For her, different sites are for different types of communication, as well as for different types of friends.

"I've known Mike online since I was 14," she says. "I met him completely by accident when I was looking for a Cliffs Notes-type site. For some reason, his website popped up when I was on that site, so I met him in chat on it."

She's been talking to him online off and on ever since. She has "talked with him on the phone only once or twice. I have no intention of meeting him in person." When she does talk or text on the phone, she uses these types of communication for different purposes. The former are more for short, to-the-point purposes like arranging a meeting place, the latter for more sustained, multiconversation socialising.

While MySpace too is used for multisocialising—sometimes for recording meeting minutes; sometimes for talking about the World Cup—most of the time, it's just used for hanging out. Even so, it is very purposeful, in the sense that teenagers need to do these kinds of things as they develop their own identities. None of it is as public as it looks to a parent or any other adult coming in and just browsing around.

Many Little Worlds

Of course, all this socialising isn't one-on-one. It's happening in the many social groups—tight and exclusive or random and easygoing—that form in secondary school and sixth form. It helps to think back to our own school days. We had groups of various sizes and levels of intimacy. Even then, there were "chavs" and "freaks," maybe even "geeks," but there were also Chess Club and the football team and the Drama Club. A person might've dipped into and identified with several groups, and found real support and validation in one, but the groups didn't really mix. They just coexisted. That's what it's like on MySpace (**FIGURE 2.5**).

Emma's school friends talk about school and social life in their MySpace profiles—people, events, parties and so on. These discussions are separate from the groups she has joined. Researcher Danah Boyd refers to this as "little communities. . . multiple publics" all coexisting in one giant space with zero contact—the groups children form and turn to for support and mutual learning in the process of learning about themselves.

"I found an entire community of Christian rock culture," says Boyd, "and they're hanging out on the same website [MySpace] with a whole group of gangsta kids—no interaction whatsoever. Adults come in and see and react to all this [together in one space] when there's actually nothing to react to, because [the teenagers] probably don't even know about each other."

MySpace Groups > Most Popular Groups

sort by: **newest** | most popular | **group name**

Listing 21-30 of 47842   **1   2   3   4   5   >>** of **4785**   **< Previous | Next >**

Most Popular Groups

	Italians (public group) This group is for the best of the best Italians. Because we do everything better	**Join Group** **Founded:** Jul 12, 2004 **Members:** 9,557
	Realest Hip Hop Heads (public group) realest hip hop heads :] 'nough said.	**Join Group** **Founded:** Jun 13, 2004 **Members:** 9,295
	Goth (private group) goth	**Join Group** **Founded:** Jun 9, 2004 **Members:** 9,111
	RaVeRs R Us (public group)	**Join Group** **Founded:** Jun 4, 2004 **Members:** 8,161
	Asian Wonderland (public group) A place for anyone who loves Asian culture and all the wonderful things that come from it!!	**Join Group** **Founded:** Jan 4, 2005 **Members:** 7,968
	Guidos and Guidettes (public group) a group for all the sexy guidos n guidettes all across the world lol	**Join Group** **Founded:** Jan 22, 2005

FIGURE 2.5 MySpace has thousands upon thousands of social groups of every imaginable makeup.

Mum and Dad might browse the profiles of kids who go to Emma's school. They might see some pretty racy or compromising party photos and think, "Look at these people our daughter is associating with!" Yet more than likely, Emma is not socialising with them at all. Her profile's just on the same site as theirs. That doesn't mean they'd be in the same *physical* space together. It's possible that they could be at the same place on a Saturday night, but for the sake of rational parent–child communication, it would work better (and be more realistic) if Emma's parents didn't make that assumption.

What we're seeing when we browse MySpace is a *whole lot* of the little communities that teenagers naturally form, try out, and sometimes depend on as they work out who they are. Young people are very focused on these communities as they socialise online, and this is a much safer way to use MySpace than the way adults approach it or think that teenagers approach it.

Acting Up in Public

Believe it or not, something MySpace reminds us of (and we're dating ourselves here) is the school canteen in *Grange Hill*, the BBC's long-running children's drama series.

Just to remind you if you weren't a fan, *Grange Hill* was one of the first TV series to present children's lives realistically—at least, as realistically as it could for a show on BBC1 at teatime—and the canteen was where Tucker, Trisha, Zammo and Roland ate, chatted, flirted and fought. The teachers and dinnerladies were there too, of course, but they generally minded their own business—the teenagers were the ones who counted.

This naturally egocentric, nothing-else-exists teenage approach lives on in the 21st century—the age of exposure. But now, many people are watching young people behave as though nothing else exists. It's a contradiction, and a very interesting one: consciously, today's teenagers seem to think that no one is out there watching, but at the subconscious level, they put on a lot of performances for that nonaudience.

The explanation might be the media environment they've grown up in. Consider the amazing time we live in. "Paris Hilton is famous because she's famous," Danah Boyd points out. The idols of *Pop Idol* are instantly famous, and the show's ratings suggest that everybody else should want to be famous, too. There are plenty more reality TV shows that are all about exposing the intimate details of people's lives—including "real" celebrities of all sorts.

"Kids are getting all these messages saying, 'Expose, expose, expose,' " Boyd says. "If you don't, your friends will expose you. We're all living in a superpublic environment, getting the message that you have more power if you expose yourself than if someone else exposes you."

You can make a fairly direct correspondence between *Pop Idol* and MySpace when you consider photo rankings and how important the number of comments and the length of friends lists can be. MySpace is just a reflection of the everyday media environment.

That's not to say every teenager likes that environment. A MySpace user posted in our forum, BlogSafety.com, that she found it "really boring—just a big popularity contest." She was referring to the vying to be among friends' "Top 8," the photo rankings, the cachet of having long friends lists and lots of comments, and so on (**FIGURE 2.6**). She left MySpace. Other dissenters just ignore this aspect of the site and get on with keeping up with the busy lives of their friends.

FIGURE 2.6 Another exhaustive friends' list on MySpace.

Our point is that MySpace is the new town centre, only infinitely bigger and more diverse. The same stuff is going on. But instead of one or two social groups, there are thousands upon thousands, and instead of an ignored group of adults passing through, there are tens of millions, both on MySpace and looking in on it.

Are They Overexposed?

Of course that's the fear: our teenagers are way overexposed as they socialise on the Net. But think for a moment about the atmosphere in which we're all living right now and how that might be shaping our thoughts about kids on MySpace.

There's a "war on terrorism" going on. Reportedly, there's a pandemic approaching. In the spring of 2006, television couldn't seem to stop showing programmes featuring sexual predators, while tabloid and broadsheet papers were beginning to pick up on the trend and running stories about predators on MySpace. We need to remember that for the editors of the *Daily Mail* and *News of the World*, MySpace and other social-networking sites are good for generating headlines like "Paedophile warning over teen websites" (*Daily Mail*, July 3, 2006). It's a good idea to take what the news media and politicians say about social networking with a good-sized pinch of salt.

"Fear is a very important emotion," says Danah Boyd, who is often quoted as someone trying to *assuage* fears. It alerts us to risk, she adds, "and how to assess it." That's true for everybody, but psychologists tell us it's also one of the principal tasks of adolescent development: risk assessment. It's something they need to do.

Even so, every generation of parents wishes it could eliminate all risk from children's lives. And every generation engages in behaviours that make parents have that wish.

A few generations ago, parents fretted over the waltz. In the 1950s, parents worried about the sexually charged influence of rock 'n' roll. Parents in the 1960s worried that experimentation with marijuana would lead their kids into lives of depravity, but somehow those kids not only survived but also managed to grow up to run companies, universities, media empires, and the country itself.

We're not being cavalier. We're just saying that social networking is today's fear of choice. But as in every generation, despite a few casualties, the vast majority of these "users" of a different sort are not being harmed even emotionally, much less physically.

We suspect that today's young people will survive this new "threat." In fact, we're confident that the positive aspects of social networking far outweigh the dangers, and based on what we now see among secondary school and sixth-form students, it's clear to us that the vast majority of kids using these sites will be just fine.

And they'll be in even better shape if they consider one important caveat: if teenagers are still in denial about the social networks being their own space, they need to come out of denial. Increasingly, university admissions offices, prospective employers, and other people whom they want to impress are searching MySpace and other such sites—not just general Web search engines—for information about them.

What young people put in their profiles and blogs can not only be found by people other than their friends, it can be printed out and filed online and on hard drives, passed along in emails and IMs, and copied and shared on file-sharing networks or third-party websites (more about this in Chapter 5). Social networkers will soon need spin-doctor skills as they negotiate this "superpublic" cyberspace.

CHAPTER 3

MySpace for Parents

Now it's time to actually try out MySpace. We don't expect most parents to become diehard MySpace fanatics (though some might), but we do hope that you'll at least sign up (it's free), create a profile, and check out a few of the features so you can see what's going on.

This chapter takes a hands-on, "cookbook" approach to using MySpace. We hope it will help you understand what the different features do and why people use them, while injecting some cautionary notes. Some of the things we'll show you include basics like how to set up a MySpace account, how to build and edit a profile, how to integrate music and video into your profile, and how to use MySpace's privacy features.

The idea, here, is for parents to get enough of a feel for the service to better understand how their children are using it and advise them on safe, smart socialising. Although we do walk you through everything you need to know to use the service (and even make it sing and dance a little), we'll be the first to admit that this book probably won't turn the average parent into a highly sophisticated MySpace user. That's not our goal.

Our goal is to help you get your feet wet, splash around the pool, have a little fun, and maybe swim a lap or two. After all, if your kids are going to be swimming in the deep end, you should know the layout of the pool.

In Chapter 4, we cover some of the ways MySpace helps manage a user's social life. Then, in Chapter 7, we take you on a tour of some of MySpace's more advanced features. Don't worry—there won't be a test, and we don't expect you to master every feature we talk about!

Setting Up an Account

Setting up a basic MySpace account is fast and easy. Follow these steps.

1. On the www.myspace.com home page, click SignUp in the top-right corner (**FIGURE 3.1**).

    This takes you directly to the signup page (**FIGURE 3.2**).

2. Provide your email address, first and last name, date of birth, gender, country, and county. Choose "UK.myspace.com-English".

    Your email address and last name won't appear in your public profile automatically, but your first name, age, and location will unless you delete them later. (We'll show you how.)

3. Create a unique password with six or more characters, containing at least one number or punctuation character.

4. Agree to comply with basic site-security protocols and the terms of the site by checking the appropriate check box.

5. Enter the characters displayed in the Verification box.

    You may have trouble deciphering the verification text, but if you get it wrong, MySpace will display a different one for you to try again.

6. Click the SignUp button.

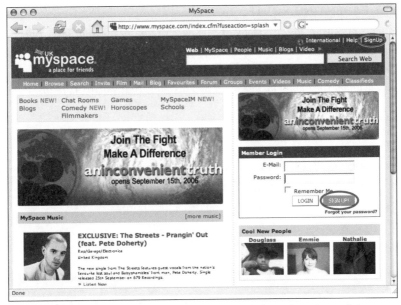

FIGURE 3.1 To sign up, click the orange button on the right side or click SignUp in the top-right corner.

FIGURE 3.2 The signup page.

KEY PARENTING POINT

*Parents may want to take a look at MySpace's terms of use and safety tips,
and go over them with their kids. MySpace is getting more responsive to
complaints about violations of these terms, including deleting the accounts of
people under the minimum age of 14 and accounts that violate its terms.*

Uploading a Photo

The next step is uploading a photo to your MySpace profile. Or you can
choose to skip this step until later by selecting the Skip for Now link at the
bottom of the page (**FIGURE 3.3**). See "Turning MySpace into YourSpace"
later in this chapter if you want to upload your photo later.

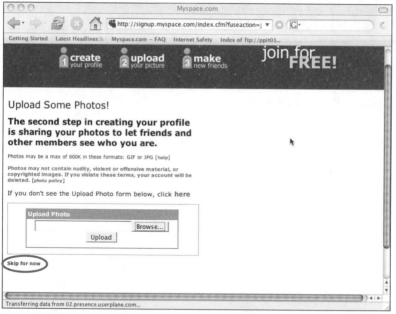

FIGURE 3.3 Here, you can upload a photo or click Skip for now to do it later.

If you have a good digital picture readily available on your computer,
you can upload it this way.

1. Click Browse to navigate to the folder on your computer's hard drive
   where you store pictures.

2. Double-click the photo you want to use.

3. Click Upload.

   It may take a minute or so for the photo to be uploaded from your hard drive to MySpace.

   Note: See "Turning MySpace into YourSpace" later in this chapter for more about photos, including some safety warnings and instructions on changing your photo or adding a caption.

KEY PARENTING POINT

Be sure that you and your kids read the MySpace safety tips, and remind them that any picture that gets posted can be seen and copied by anyone who has access to the profile. It can also be saved and passed around the Internet even after your child deletes it. Ask your son or daughter how he or she would feel if the photos were seen by university admissions departments, future employers, or Aunt Sophie.

Inviting Friends

Before you can view your new basic profile, you'll be asked to share your new page and invite your friends to MySpace (**FIGURE 3.4**). You can choose

FIGURE 3.4 You can invite friends during setup or click Skip for now to do it later.

to notify your contacts by following the address-input instructions or skip
this step until later.

The Hello Page

Congratulations—your new MySpace account is active! The Hello page
essentially is your MySpace home page and central site-navigation tool.
Your home page is unique, and it's different from MySpace's main home
pages at www.myspace.com and uk.myspace.com.

You can access your home page by clicking Home in the menu
near the top of any screen in MySpace. To get to the *site's* main home
page, click the MySpace.com link in the top corner of any screen
(**FIGURE 3.5**).

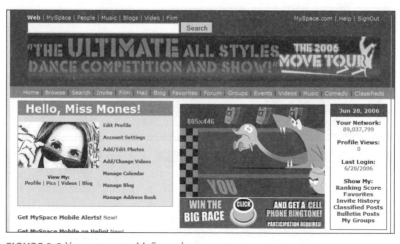

FIGURE 3.5 Your very own MySpace home page.

Every time you log in with your user name and password, you'll
be autodirected to your home page. Your home page is your
jumping-off point for editing or enhancing your profile. Only you
have access to this page. Though it looks a lot like what the public sees,
it's actually a little different. The URL of the page the public will see
is displayed in the box that says "Tell people about your MySpace"
(**FIGURE 3.6**).

```
                                                    Help
           Pick your MySpace Name/URL!
                    Click Here

          Tell people about your MySpace [?]

                        My URL
          http://www.myspace.com/84395566

                      My Blog URL
           http://blog.myspace.com/84395566

          Make MySpace my Home Page
```

FIGURE 3.6 Here's where you can choose a URL that isn't a bunch of mind-numbing numbers.

Getting a Friendly MySpace URL

The web address (URL) in the "Tell people about your MySpace" area probably looks something like http://www.myspace.com/ 84395566. Unless your friends have good heads for numbers, none of them will remember that. Fortunately, just below that listing is a box that says "Pick your MySpace Name/URL!" If you click that box, you can replace those numbers with something people can remember. If your choice has already been used by another member, you'll get an error message and a chance to try a different word.

By the way, in case you were wondering, *URL* stands for *uniform resource locator*. Don't you just love techie terms?

There actually is an upside and a downside to an all-numbers URL. If an address is harder to remember, it's also harder to find—whether the finder is a parent or someone with bad intentions. It's a good talking point for parents and children.

Your MySpace home page has several features and tools, some of which we will highlight in this section and expand on in greater detail later in this chapter.

Up to this point, you've provided only basic profile information, so your home page looks pretty sparse. The steps in the following sections let you flesh out your profile by providing details.

KEY PARENTING POINT

For privacy and protection, especially if you log into MySpace on public or shared computers, we recommend that you and your family follow certain practices when logging in and out. When signing in to MySpace (or any password-requiring site), make sure that the "Remember Me" box remains unchecked. When you're finished using MySpace, log out completely by clicking Sign Out in the top-right corner of any screen. We provide more information about passwords in Chapter 5.

MySpace: Subject to Change without Notice

As this book was going to press, the Hello box went through some changes. We think we caught it in time, but it reminded us that MySpace can change at any moment. It's not likely to change radically on any given day, but the company does tweak the interface now and then, which can affect how you use the service. If you come across a discrepancy between our instructions and what you see on the screen, don't blame us—in fact—don't blame anyone. That's the nature of the Web.

Also keep in mind that if something doesn't work right, it might not be your fault. It could be a bug, as we discovered when reviewing a couple of new features. That's a price we pay for living on the cutting edge. But we have good news—we guess: this book is set in stone, and until the next edition, it won't change.

Personalising Your Profile

MySpace requires only basic information to create and maintain a user account. But as you cruise around the site, you'll notice that most users—especially teenagers—add a great deal of detail and personality. The more information they share, of course, the more information they're giving out to the general public, which is why in Chapter 5 we advise parents to remind children to be very careful about the type of information they put out there.

To add to your profile, click the Edit Profile link in the blue box in the top-left corner of your home page (**FIGURE 3.7**).

FIGURE 3.7 Click the Edit Profile link.

The Profile Edit–Interests & Personality page appears (**FIGURE 3.8**). This is where you begin adding information about yourself. Other categories for adding information, such as Name, Basic Info, and Background & Lifestyle can be accessed using the tabs at the top of the page.

Note that you have full ownership of your profile and are free to answer questions and fill in boxes (or not), as you wish. If you don't feel comfortable answering certain questions, don't bother. When MySpace loads your profile, it will show only populated fields. Questions and categories left blank will be invisible. A few fields, however, will be filled in automatically.

In most cases, you have the option to delete or change the automatically populated fields. You can change your display name, for example (by default, it's your first name), or remove or change the name of your town. You can

FIGURE 3.8 The Profile Edit page, where you can write anything about yourself in the boxes beside the headings.

even change your gender (well, what you say is your gender) and your date of birth. See the section "Adding a display name" for details on how to do this.

Adding Interests and Personality Details

The Profile Edit–Interests & Personality page (**FIGURE 3.8**) has text boxes that allow creative expression, including, from some teenage users, information that probably shouldn't be there. You can leave any of these boxes blank, or you can type anything you want the public to see. As we explain in Chapter 7, some people even add HTML to some of these boxes to enhance (or mess up) their pages.

Note: Don't worry too much about HTML; you don't have to use it, and even if you do decide to use it, you don't have to know much about it, as we'll explain in Chapter 7.

Your browser will be directed to this page after you've set up your account. If you want to alter this page later, you can access it by clicking the Edit Profile link in the Hello box on your home page.

You can add anything from short 'n' sweet comments to lengthy descriptions and details.

- **Headline.** The headline is a short, simple statement or personal handle.
- **About Me.** This section is for your personal bio or statement—a verbal snapshot of who you are. Content here varies greatly, from funny, interesting, and succinct to obnoxiously verbose to pure, unintelligible slang.
- **I'd Like to Meet.** You can list specific people you'd like to meet (celebrities, historic figures, athletes), groups (such as a band or team), or general types of people.
- **Interests.** Here, you present information about what makes you tick, such as hobbies, interests, activities, and joys (**FIGURE 3.9**).
- **Music.** Music has its own category because it's such a big personality piece. You can learn a lot about people based on their musical tastes, and MySpace users have the option to express and define themselves by providing detail about their musical likes and dislikes.
- **Movies, Television, and Books.** MySpace users can elaborate further on their entertainment likes and dislikes in these sections.
- **Heroes.** Typically, users put the name of a real or fictional person here, but many people skip this question.

Keeping It Safe

It's important for children to know that they don't have to answer all the questions that appear on the Profile Edit pages, given the personal nature of these details. Although 22-year-old adults might feel comfortable disclosing their sexual preferences, drinking/smoking preferences, or where they went to school, such details may be unnecessary, inappropriate, or even unsafe for a teenager. MySpace has restrictions on inappropriate language and images. Threatening, violent, or explicit content is unacceptable, and MySpace will delete accounts it discovers that are in violation of these restrictions.
For better or worse, however, most of the millions of profiles are unregulated, and users are able to express themselves freely.

Miss Mones's Interests	
General	Reading, writing, music, travel, soccer, yoga/pilates, cooking, long outdoor walks, dancing, biking, films, good food and drink, great company/conversation...hanging out with friends, kitties, copyediting, German, comedy, and Trader Joes.
Music	Styles: Alt./Rock, Lounge, Trip-Hop/Acid Jazz, 80's. Bands/Artists: U2, Tori Amos, Hooverphonic, Beck, Radiohead, Coldplay, Massive Attack, Gomez, The Shins, Interpol, The Postal Service, Franz Ferdinand, Miles End, lounge music. New likes: The Lovemakers, The Killers, Death Cab for Cutie, Pinback. Old faves: Beatles, Led Zepplin, Depeche Mode, Garbage, Cranberries, The Cure.
Movies	The Princess Bride and many more!
Television	24, Grey's Anatomy, Sex and the City, The Family Guy, The Simpsons
Books	Right now I'm reading The Beach by Alex Garland.
Heroes	Bono

FIGURE 3.9 The interests page is how you represent yourself online.

Adding a Display Name

MySpace recommends you create a "display name" for your profile (elsewhere known as a screenname). That's your MySpace nickname and can be anything you want—your first name, nickname, or any other label.

1. At the top of the Profile Edit–Interests & Personality page, click the Name link.

   The Profile Edit–Name page appears. On this page, you're likely to see the name you entered when you signed up.

2. Leave the display name as it is, or type a different one (**FIGURE 3.10**).

3. Click Save Changes.

FIGURE 3.10 Your display or screen name: how everybody identifies you on MySpace.

Your display name won't show up in your profile but will be stored in the MySpace database, allowing other users who know your name to search for you. For complete anonymity, you can opt to fill in only the display name and delete your last name if it's there by default. This makes it more difficult for friends to find you on MySpace, which is something many teenagers want to avoid.

KEY PARENTING POINT

We recommend that all users, teenage and adult, consider using nicknames and other names for privacy—and at the very least not to use last names. It's also a good idea, especially for teenagers, to avoid nicknames that are sexually suggestive.

Adding Background and Lifestyle Details

To access this page, click the Background & Lifestyle link at the top of any of the Profile Edit pages.

The majority of questions on this page are purely optional; again, parents can remind their children that they don't need to answer all the questions. Users can reveal more information about themselves by checking applicable selections for:

- marital status (not optional)
- sexual orientation (see below)
- home town
- religion
- smoker
- drinker
- children
- education
- income.

KEY PARENTING POINT

A lot of people use MySpace and other social networks to seek out a potential romantic interest or just to flirt—which, we suppose, is why MySpace asks about sexual orientation. But before young people check this box and provide more detail, have them consider the consequences. Ask whether it's really necessary to give out this information. We suspect that most teenagers would answer "yes," but it's this type of information that a potential predator will look at.

The option that concerns us the most is "not sure," because a predator could interpret that comment as coming from a someone who is insecure about his or her sexuality. We feel that the default option, "no answer," is a safer choice.

Including School Information

Almost all children list the name of their school. We prefer that youngsters don't give out that information, because it does help predators locate them. Actually, though, this cat is already out of the bag. The whole point of social networking is to help people find one another—ideally, people they know from the real world.

Children's lives revolve around school and, given the culture of MySpace, there's almost no way to persuade most teenagers not to reveal their school name, because it helps them find classmates. This, by itself, is one of the positive and safe aspects of the service. Assuming that young people do give out their school name, the key is to avoid giving out too much other information, as we discuss throughout this book.

But this advice isn't just for children. In addition to current school, users can list former schools on the Profile Edit – Schools page, along with lots of optional information that can help former pupils find one another.

To access the Schools page, click the Schools link at the top of any Profile Edit page.

Adding Employer Information

Though this section applies mainly to adults, it can affect teenagers with part-time or summer jobs as well. Users can include former and current employers in their profile. This can provide opportunities to network and socialise with co-workers, but it also makes it easier for an employer to find your profile. There have been cases in which employees have been fired (and students disciplined) as a result of postings that the employer or school considered to be inappropriate, illegal, or in violation of policy. Parents can help children remember that.

To access this page, click the Companies link at the top of any Profile Edit page.

Listing Areas of Interest for Networking

MySpace is a social network that many people use to reach out to others with similar interests. These interests can be business-related, political, artistic, or purely social. There are other places in the service (including groups) where you can find like-minded people, but by specifying your networking interests, you can make it easier for people with similar interests to find you.

You can also select networking categories in specific fields and industries to add to your profile.

If you display your networking interests in your profile, other writers, dancers, or marketing people on MySpace can find you when they search for people with a specific affiliation.

To access the page, click the Networking link at the top of any Profile Edit page.

After you've added all the details about yourself to your profile, click the View My Profile link in the top-right corner of the page to preview your profile (**FIGURE 3.11**).

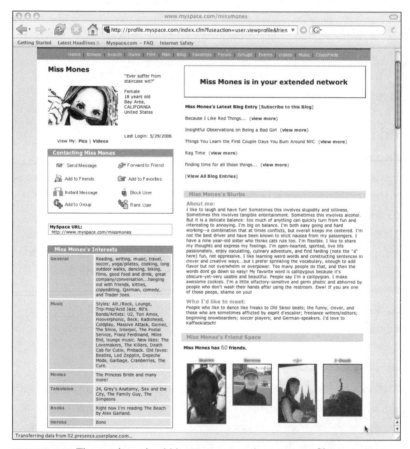

FIGURE 3.11 The results at last! Now you can review your profile.

TIP

It's also a good idea to view your home page as others will see it, using the public URL, and then change anything you feel is inappropriate, ugly, or just plain stupid (not that parents ever do stupid things).

Setting Privacy Options

MySpace gives you some control of how other people can find you, contact you, and view or comment on your profile. In most cases, MySpace sets the default privacy settings to the least private options (except for people who are 14 or 15 years old, whose accounts can be viewed either by friends only or by anyone younger than 18 on MySpace).

In summer 2006, MySpace announced that all MySpace users have the option of making their profiles private. Prior to this, private profiles were available only to 14- and 15-year-olds. The default settings for users who register as being 16 or older are likely to remain public, so it's still a good idea to customise the privacy settings to a level that's comfortable for you or your child.

MySpace Privacy: A Moving Target

MySpace changed its privacy options in late June 2006. When we learned of the news, we contacted a company official, who stated the obvious: "These types of changes can happen at any time, as our site is a work in progress." She added, "This is the problem with putting things down in print about the Internet—change happens so very fast."

It appears MySpace changed its privacy options in two significant ways. First, all users—not just 14- and 15-year-olds—have the option to make their profiles private. Second, new restrictions have been imposed on how adults can contact users under 16. Under the new rules, MySpace users who are 18 or older can no longer send a request to be on the friends list of a 14- or 15-year-old unless the adult already knows the user's full name or email address.

Of course, all of these changes to MySpace's privacy options are based on "the honour system." Until reliable age verification technology is developed and implemented, a child under 16 can register as being older, and an adult can pose as a teenager.

KEY PARENTING POINT

Setting a young person's profile so that it can be read by anyone younger than 18 on MySpace hides the profile from only those people who say they're 18 or older. Because there is no age-verification process, it's possible for adults to say they're under 18 and still view these profiles. Also, even a private profile can be searched. The full profile won't be displayed, but some basic information can be viewed.

To view or make changes to your privacy settings, follow these steps.

1. On your MySpace home page, click the Account Settings link (**FIGURE 3.12**).

FIGURE 3.12 Click Account Settings to display your privacy options.

2. Scroll down to Privacy Settings, and select Change Settings.
3. To change certain settings, simply check the applicable check boxes and then click Change Settings (**FIGURE 3.13**).

Choices include the following.

- **Require Email or Last Name to Add Me As a Friend.** This setting gives you a little more privacy by preventing people from adding you as

My Privacy Settings	
☐	Require email or last name to add me as a friend
☐	Approve Comments before Posting
☐	Hide Online Now
☑	Show My Birthday to my Friends
☐	No Pic Forwarding
☐	Friend Only Blog Comments
☐	Block Friend Request From Bands
☐	Friend Only Group Invites
☐	Disable Band Songs From Automatically Starting
Who Can View My Full Profile	
○	My Friends Only
◉	Public

Change Settings   Cancel

FIGURE 3.13 Select the privacy options you want.

a friend unless they know your email address or last name. To add you, they have to know at least a little bit about you.

- **Approve Comments Before Posting.** By default, any of your MySpace friends can post comments to your profile page. Such comments can be embarrassing or could violate your privacy. Although you can delete them later, the comments will stay there until you do. It's a smart idea to tick this check box, because it gives you the power to approve comments before they're posted. The only downside is that friends who post comments have to wait a while before the world can see them. But others can't post malicious or just stupid comments to your page.

- **Hide Online Now.** By default, other MySpace users can tell if you're online. That can be handy if they want to send you an instant message, but you may not want to tell the world that you or your children are sitting at a computer using MySpace at this very moment (it's a pretty good clue that you're home, which you may not want others to know). Selecting this check box hides that display.

- **Show My Birthday to My Friends.** This option (checked by default) tells your friends that it's time to send you a gift or at least a "Happy birthday" greeting. It's relatively safe, but birthdays are one of many pieces of information that identity thieves use.

- **No Pic Forwarding.** If you turn this option off, you're preventing other users from emailing your photo to any MySpace user they choose. Not allowing picture forwarding gives you only a little more control of your picture—people with a little more tech know-how can still copy your photo and paste it wherever they want. But even a little bit of control helps.

- **Friend Only Blog Comments.** By default, anyone can post to your blog. This option limits blog postings to friends only. As we discuss in "Blogging" in Chapter 4, a blog is separate from your basic profile; many MySpace users don't use blogs.

- **Block Friend Request from Bands.** As we said earlier, music is the soul of MySpace, and it's set up for bands and fans to connect, which is why a lot of people like to include bands as their "friends." The downside, however, is that you could get unwanted email from bands you don't want to hear from, so selecting this option means that bands can't send you requests to be among your friends. Even if you block these requests, you can still initiate contact with bands and add them as your friends.

- **Friend Only Group Invites.** MySpace groups enable people to invite others to join them to discuss a variety of topics. But you may get more invitations than you bargained for, so when you choose this option, you get invitations only from your friends.

- **Disable Band Songs from Automatically Starting.** This setting is more for your sanity and peace of mind than for your privacy. As you surf around MySpace, you'll hear a lot of music, whether you want to or not. Sometimes, it can be distracting. So by selecting this option, you won't hear the music.

When you are registered with MySpace as being 16 years old or older, the Who Can View My Full Profile section at the bottom of the privacy settings window provides two options:

- **My Friends Only.** Only the people on a person's friends list can view the profile.

- **Public.** The profile can be viewed by anyone. This is the default option, so it has to be changed if you or your teenager want more control.

When children are registered with MySpace as being 14 or 15 years old, the Who Can View My Full Profile section at the bottom of the privacy settings window provides a different set of options (**FIGURE 3.14**):

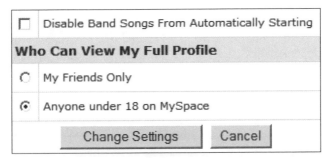

FIGURE 3.14 These extra privacy options are only for people who register as being 14 or 15 years old.

- **My Friends Only.** Only the people on a person's friends list can view the profile.

- **Anyone Under 18 on MySpace.** Only MySpace users who say they are 18 years old or younger can view the profile. This is the default option.

Note: What you see onscreen may look different from Figure 3.14, since MySpace is constantly reviewing its privacy policy. Keep in mind that the settings could change further as MySpace rolls out additional privacy settings.

Adjusting Other Account Settings

In addition to privacy settings, MySpace has extensive account settings that let you customise your account and profile. You can change your email address. You can prevent MySpace from sending notices to your usual email account (not your MySpace account).

Just click any category you want to explore or change in your Hello box, including Privacy Settings (see the preceding section), IM Privacy Settings, Mobile Settings, Group Settings, Calendar Settings, Blocked Users, Profile Views, Profile Settings, Music Settings, and Away Messages.

When you click any of these categories, you'll see an explanation of what it does and how you can change it (**FIGURE 3.15**).

FIGURE 3.15 Click the text in red to change settings in a category.

Making adjustments or changing settings in all these categories is a lot like the profile-management process we walked you through earlier in this chapter. You may notice an option called Mobile Settings, however. This option determines how users can access MySpace with their mobile phones. At the moment this is only available in the US but it is likely to be extended.

To make any adjustments, follow these steps:

1. On your MySpace home page, click the Account Settings link in your Hello box (**FIGURE 3.5**).

2. Explore your options, view the help messages MySpace provides with them, and make any appropriate changes.

The rest of this section gives you specifics on some settings of particular interest to parents of MySpace users.

Blocking Users

The Blocked Users feature lets you view and unblock the users or groups that were blocked previously. (This is not the area where you can initially block a user. To do that, you must visit that user's profile and click Block User in the Contacting section just beneath the profile photo.)

The Block User feature is sort of a cross between a spam filter and a digital restraining order. Blocked users can still view your profile, but they cannot send you a message or communicate with you.

KEY PARENTING POINT

Some users "hack" their profile to obscure or de-emphasise this box, making it hard to find the block feature. For more details about hacks and advanced profile design, see Chapter 7.

Profile Settings

These settings give you control of some of the information others can see in your profile, as well as whether they can use HTML in comments that appear in your profile.

We talk more about HTML in Chapter 7, but in short, HTML is simple computer code that gives people a great deal of control not only of how things look in a profile, but also of how they act (flashing text, special fonts, sounds, graphics, and so on).

Poorly written HTML can cause MySpace and your browser to crash and can even crash your computer or—in theory—violate your privacy. By default (at this writing), MySpace lets users post HTML comments on your page. That can make your page look very cool, but it can also cause problems. Disabling the ability for others to add HTML to your page can prevent these types of problems.

To change the HTML Comments option, follow these steps.

1. Click Change Settings in Profile Settings.

2. If you want your friends and other MySpace users to know what groups you are interested in, check the Display Groups I Belong To check box (**FIGURE 3.16**).

    Each name of a MySpace group that you belong to will be displayed as a text link in the My Groups section of your profile.

My Profile Settings

☑	Display Groups I belong to
☐	Disable HTML Profile Comments
☐	Disable HTML In Pic Comments
☐	Disable HTML In Blog Comments

Change Settings | Cancel

FIGURE 3.16 Displaying your groups shows people more about your interests and affiliations.

3. If you want to prevent people from posting images in the comments section of your profile, check Disable HTML Profile Comments.

4. When you finish making your selections, click the Change Settings button.

KEY PARENTING POINT

Because HTML is a programming language, it's possible to use it to do a lot. This includes linking to other websites and embedding in MySpace pages images and video that are actually stored on other sites—in other words, photos and clips that may violate MySpace's rules and harm users' computers or jeopardise their privacy, despite the fact that MySpace takes steps to minimise these risks. Urge your children to be very careful about using HTML, including code that they paste in from other sites. For more information about HTML, see Chapter 7.

Music Settings

These settings can help you control the way the music player works when people access your profile or when you access other people's profiles.

Music is an integral part of teenagers' identity and culture, which is why a lot of them not only use it in their profiles, but also configure it to play automatically when people go there. Still, sometimes silence really is golden, which is why MySpace gives users to the option of disabling music from starting automatically when you visit other people's profiles and when they visit yours.

To view or change the music settings, follow these steps.

1. Click Change Settings.

2. To prevent the music player from playing when people view your profile, check Disable My Player from Automatically Starting.

TIP

If visitors want to hear the music, they can start it manually by clicking the play button in the music player.

3. To prevent music from playing automatically as you browse other people's profiles, check Disable Band Songs from Automatically Starting.

4. Click the Change Settings button to save your changes.

In "Turning MySpace into YourSpace," later in this chapter, we'll tell you how to add music to your profile.

Away Message

If you plan to be away from your computer or just off MySpace for a while (which we think is a good idea from time to time!), you can display an away message that people will get when they send you a message. By default, there is no such message in MySpace, but you can click on Edit Away Message in Account Settings to create one (**FIGURE 3.17**). Make sure that you save your message when you finish writing it.

KEY PARENTING POINT

Children can get very creative with their away messages, which can be fun, but caution your teenagers not to use the away message to reveal anything inappropriate, including where they plan to be while away from the computer.

FIGURE 3.17 Here's where you explain where you're off to.

Turning MySpace Into YourSpace

As you navigate MySpace and check out profiles, you'll notice that the look and feel varies tremendously from user to user. Some people have profiles with a personalised description, unique photos, and perhaps a little extra here and there; others have decked out their pages with crazy fonts, glitzy wallpaper, music, and video graphics (**FIGURE 3.18**). You don't have to do any of this fancy customising, but if you are curious about how it's done, check out Chapter 7.

FIGURE 3.18 One of the more souped-up profiles we've seen.

Photos

People are visual creatures so, naturally, they want to look at pictures. The popular MySpace photo feature lets you upload up to eight digital photos or images (including your profile image) to your profile. Photos let you share more about yourself and your life, including friends, family members, and pets.

You can upload virtually any image: artwork, graphics, illustrations, cartoons, pictures, and other images. All photos must be in .gif or .jpg format and no larger than 600 KB.

MySpace users often experiment and add a creative touch to their profiles by using popular or unique images in their profiles rather than traditional photographs or portraits. This can provide added privacy protection, too, but make sure that you and your children know not to violate MySpace rules and copyright law by posting other people's images without permission.

MySpace also prohibits photos that "contain nudity, violent or offensive material." Warn your children that MySpace will delete their accounts if it catches them violating these terms.

Company policy and basic courtesy also prohibit uploading images of other people without their permission.

KEY PARENTING POINT

If you or your child come across photos that you believe violate these policies, you can report them to MySpace by clicking the Report This Image link below each photo you see in people's profiles. In Chapter 5, we talk more about photos and how to identify and report child pornography.

Sometimes, images or videos are actually stored on another site (as we mentioned in our discussion of HTML earlier in this chapter); they're not on MySpace at all. But because MySpace lets users add HTML to their profiles, users can add links to media at sites like Photobucket.com and YouTube.com.

Note: MySpace says it's negotiating with some of these sites to police the storage of media files that violate its terms, but that's a tall order, because media-storage and media-sharing sites are multiplying rapidly on Web 2.0.

If you didn't upload a photo when you created your MySpace account, you can always do it now.

To upload a photo, follow these steps.

1. Click the Add/Edit Photos link in the Hello box on your home page (**FIGURE 3.19**).

FIGURE 3.19 The Add/Edit Photos option.

2. Click Browse, which lets you navigate to the folder on your computer's hard drive where you store pictures.

3. Double-click the photo you want to use.

4. Click Upload.

    It may take a minute or so for the photo to be uploaded from your hard drive to MySpace.

You can opt to include a caption with the photo. You can do that from the same screen where you uploaded the photo, or you can do it later by clicking the Add/Edit Photos link on your home page.

To add a caption, follow these steps.

1. Scroll down to the bottom of the Upload Your Photo page where your photo appears, and click Add Caption below the photo.

2. Write your caption in the text box.

3. Click Update Caption.

    A Confirm Caption screen displays.

4. If you're satisfied with the caption, click Post Caption; otherwise, click the Back button, and make changes.

<u>KEY PARENTING POINT</u>

Although MySpace prohibits nude photos, it doesn't necessarily censor photos that could be suggestive or otherwise inappropriate. Teenagers may need reminding that their photos can have an impact on how people perceive those who are depicted in them, whether it's themselves, their friends, or family members (some parents have been dismayed to find unflattering pictures of themselves in their childrens' profiles). Photos can also easily be copied and pasted into others' Web pages and sent around via email. So once the photos are posted, their owners have little control over them. Ideally, it's best that the photos at least not clearly identify the young people in them, though that may be a tough sell, considering the millions of photos on the service that do just that.

Adding Music to Your Profile

A lot of young people display their "music personality" by uploading a song to play automatically when people visit their profile and changing it often. Unlike some services, MySpace allows users to upload songs only from bands that are already on the service. You can't upload MP3 or iTunes files from your own collection. This is MySpace's way of promoting its member bands and trying to make sure that users don't upload copyrighted music without permission.

To upload a profile song, follow these steps.

1. In your Hello box, click the Edit Profile link.

2. Click the Profile Songs link (**FIGURE 3.20**).
    The Add a Song to Your Profile page displays.

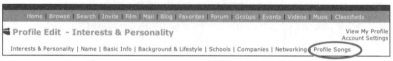

FIGURE 3.20 Profile songs is the last Profile Edit option on the right.

3. To start searching for a song, click Find a Band in MySpace Music (**FIGURE 3.21**).

4. Enter the band name in the keyword search box, and click Search. At least one band profile appears.

FIGURE 3.21 Browse for a tune by clicking the blue text.

5. Select the appropriate profile by clicking the band's name (**FIGURE 3.22**). A song most likely will start playing automatically.

6. Choose the song that's playing or another song, and click Add. A confirmation page appears, asking whether you're sure you want to add the song to your profile.

7. Click the Add Song to Profile button (**FIGURE 3.23**). A final band-upload confirmation screen appears (**FIGURE 3.24**).

Voilà! You've added tunes to your MySpace profile.

To remove a song from your profile, follow these steps.

1. Complete steps 1 and 2 in the preceding list.

2. Click Remove next to the song and artist you want to remove.

Adding Video to Your Profile

Similar to MySpace Music, the Videos feature lets users share their favourite clips and shorts directly in their profiles. You can see these

FIGURE 3.22 Choose a band's profile to check out its songs.

FIGURE 3.23 Choose a song and then add it to your profile.

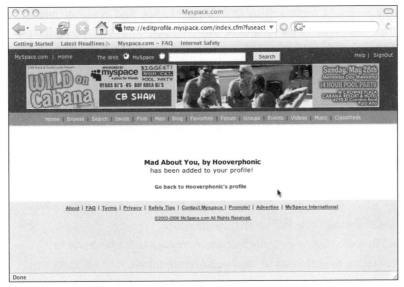

FIGURE 3.24 Your tune choice has been confirmed.

videos playing when you visit profiles, and sometimes, you can see several videos at the same time, which can be a real challenge for grownup eyes. Still, these videos are very important to the way young people present themselves, and they're a very popular feature on the service.

It's also possible to upload home videos to a home page. Teenagers are increasingly using camcorders or even video-enabled mobile phones to shoot their own video and then uploading it to MySpace and other video-sharing services. Many of the user-generated videos we've seen are terrific, and some are very funny. (If you really want to delve into this, check out YouTube.com and Grouper.com, two social-networking sites that specialise in video.)

KEY PARENTING POINT

Naturally, parents are going to worry about their children viewing and, especially, posting inappropriate videos. As with photos, MySpace has a strict no pornography policy and actually checks out user-supplied videos before they're posted to make sure that they don't violate the rules. That, however, is no guarantee that kids won't post homemade videos that jeopardise their own privacy, so parents still need to be on the alert. And as with all media these days, your idea of what's OK might not necessarily be the same as the MySpace policy. That's why parents—not the government or corporations—are the ultimate arbiters for their own children.

We suspect that most parents aren't going to be uploading their own video, but if you want to know how it's done, check out Chapter 7.

Calendars

MySpace has an easy-to-use calendar to help you track your schedule or your family's schedule. Children can use it to help coordinate their lives and share their calendars with their friends.

One nice family-friendly feature we really like is the ability to configure the calendar to send you a reminder via your MySpace mail, your "external" (usual email account) mail, or both. That way, you won't forget an appointment, a friend's birthday, or the date of your child's parents' evening, and maybe your children will even use it to remind themselves of important after-school practices and lessons.

You create your calendar by clicking the Manage Calendar link in the blue box on your home page, adjacent to your picture. To enter an event, click the time when the event will start, and fill out the form just as you would any computer-based calendar.

The Calendar Sharing option lets you control who can view your calendar. Select the appropriate choice from the Calendar Sharing drop-down menu (**FIGURE 3.25**). Your choices are Share with Friends (the default), Disabled (for maximum privacy), and Share with Everyone (if you want the world to know what you're doing and when).

KEY PARENTING POINT

By default, your calendar is shared with your friends, but you can disable sharing or decide to share your calendar with everyone. As you've probably guessed, the latter option generally is a bad idea, especially for teenagers, because it lets anyone know what they're doing and when they're doing it.

FIGURE 3.25 Disabling sharing is definitely the safest option.

Cancelling an Account

If you want to terminate your MySpace account, here's how.

1. Log into MySpace, and click the Account Settings link on your MySpace home page.

2. On your Account Settings page, click the Cancel Account link in red at the top of the page (see Figure 3.14).

3. On the Cancel MySpace Account page, click the Cancel My Account button (**FIGURE 3.26**).

   A confirmation email message will be sent to the email account you used to create your MySpace account (**FIGURE 3.27**).

4. Locate the email message that was sent to you, and follow the instructions in that email to delete your account.

FIGURE 3.26 Click the red "Cancel My Account" button in the Confirm Cancel Account box.

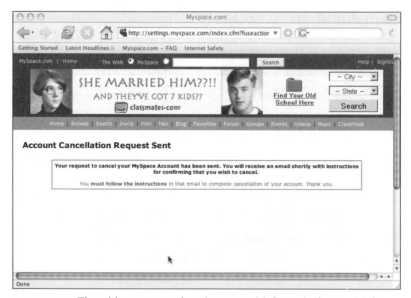

FIGURE 3.27 The address you used to sign up on MySpace is the one MySpace will send your cancellation instructions to. If the address that was used wasn't real, see the sidebar "Cancelling Your Child's Account" in Chapter 6.

TIP

MySpace warns you, "Cancelling your MySpace account will permanently remove all of your profile information from MySpace, including your photographs, comments, journals, and your personal network of friends. This information cannot be restored." Users can create a new account at any time, but may have to use a different email address (not a problem, when free email accounts can be established at Hotmail, Yahoo!, etc. at any time). Parents considering cancelling childrens' accounts might encounter strong reactions, given the social and time investments that go into these profiles.

We've covered the basics of setting up and managing a profile, which is all you really need to get started. But turn the page. In Chapter 4, we cover the all-important topic of how people are using MySpace to manage their social lives, with plenty more "hands-on" tips on how teenagers and adults can use this service.

CHAPTER 4

Managing the Social Stuff

MySpace's tagline is "a place for friends," and true to its word, the site provides numerous tools for socialising and managing a network of friends.

This chapter builds on the basic account management you learned about in Chapter 3, providing a step-by-step exploration of the tools and communities on MySpace that help young users manage the online part of their busy social lives. By getting a basic sense of how this management is done, we hope you will feel less daunted and more free to engage in your child's involvement with MySpace. Who knows? You might find it helps you manage your own online social life— except that you'll have to get your whole book group to join MySpace too!

Making and Managing Friends

We feel compelled to make a distinction between the friends you make on MySpace and the friends you actually know in the real world. As it turns out, most of the teenagers we've spoken with tell us that they use the service mainly to communicate with mates they know from school or other real-world places; to communicate with bands; or, in some cases, to communicate with people who have common interests in sports, games, politics, and other activities.

MySpace does have features that let you respond to and seek out people you meet through the service, of course. We urge that teenagers use these features cautiously, if at all. This is especially important for young people who, as we discussed in Chapter 2, sometimes use social-networking sites to collect friends, treating the service as a sort of popularity contest. Obviously, they can be more vulnerable to contacts from strangers who want to become their "friends."

MySpace tries to make it difficult for adults to view the full profiles of 14- and 15-year-old users and to contact those users, but the additional protection depends on people being honest about their ages, as we mentioned in Chapter 3. So it's still possible that your children will hear from strangers who want to be their friend.

Savvy teenage users tell us that they never add such people to their friends lists without first checking out the profiles to be sure that there is a real connection, such as a person they know from school or elsewhere who has genuine shared interests, or at least a friend of a friend. We'll have a lot more to say about social-networking safety in the next chapter.

Adding Friends

Even if you have a public profile, there are certain privileges that are available only to people you designate as "friends." For example, only friends can post on your profile, comment on your picture or see certain information. If your profile is private, it's off-limits to all but your friends. That's why, on MySpace as in life, it's important to remind your kids to choose their friends carefully.

To add a friend who isn't a MySpace user, do the following.

1. Send an invitation by clicking the Invite link on the blue navigation bar to the top of any page (**FIGURE 4.1**).

FIGURE 4.1 To invite a friend, click Invite in the blue navigation bar at the top of any MySpace page.

2. Enter your friend's email address, and type a message into the box below it (**FIGURE 4.2**).

FIGURE 4.2 Type the friends' email addresses (separated by commas) in the To text box.

You need to enter the email addresses of the friends you want to invite, separating them with a comma. Take time to make sure you've spelt them all correctly as otherwise you may send an invite to someone you don't know.

Your friends will get an email from MySpace asking them to sign up. If they don't bother signing up then nothing will happen and you won't be able to add them on MySpace.

MySpace users in the United States can import email addresses from other services like HotMail, but we think you're better off without this feature as it can easily be misused.

To add a friend who is already on MySpace.

1. On the person's profile page, click the Add to Friends link in the Contacting box (**FIGURE 4.3**).

FIGURE 4.3 Click Add to Friends in the Contacting box on the left side of the profile page.

2. MySpace will ask if you really want to add the person. If so, click the Add to Friends button (**FIGURE 4.4**).

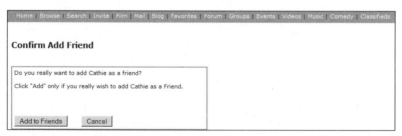

FIGURE 4.4 Click Add to Friends to confirm you really want to add that person to your friends list.

The person you're trying to add will get a "New Friend Request Message" (see the next section, "Accepting or Denying Friend Requests") and will have the option to Approve, Deny or Send you a message. If you're approved, you will show up on that person's friends list, and he or she will show up on yours.

Accepting or Denying Friend Requests

If you receive a new friend request, you'll receive notification in the My Mail section of your home page. You'll also be notified in your non-MySpace personal email account (the one you used to sign up with MySpace) if you chose in Account Settings to receive those external notifications (see "Adjusting Other Account Settings" in Chapter 3).

Friend requests, like all other notifications (Comments, Blogs, and Event Invites), are hard to miss. As soon as you log into MySpace, a little envelope and New Friend Requests! message appears in blue at the top of the My Mail area on your home page (**FIGURE 4.5**).

My Mail	
✉ New Friend Requests!	
inbox	friend requests
sent	post bulletin

FIGURE 4.5 You've got a New Friend Request!

It is common to receive MySpace friend requests from people you know, as well as from complete strangers (unless you have a private profile). All requests are pending and remain so for a month. During that time, a user can view and explore the requester's profile, and has the choice to accept the request, deny the request, or contact the requester via MySpace mail. If you choose to do nothing, the request will disappear from your inbox in 30 days, and you will not be added to the person's friends list.

To accept or deny a friend request, follow these steps.

1. In the My Mail section of your home page, click the blue New Friend Requests! Link (**FIGURE 4.4**).

   The Friend Request Manager page displays.

2. Click Approve to add the requester to your friends list, or click Deny to decline, in which case the request will be deleted from your inbox (**FIGURE 4.6**).

FIGURE 4.6 Approve or deny friend requests from this screen.

Inviters don't get any kind of notification when their requests have been denied (although they probably will figure it out when they don't end up being added to your friends list).

KEY PARENTING POINT

Don't forget: remind your children to be very cautious before accepting a request from someone they don't know in the real world—or at least register your concern, because they've probably heard it before. Even when people have very cool profiles and seem to be the type of people you'd like to get to know, that doesn't mean they are who they say they are. There have been numerous cases of people making up very convincing profiles that are totally fake.

We recommend that teenagers (and adults, too) use MySpace to hang out with people whom they truly know are who they say they are. A very good rule—especially for younger social networkers—is that their parents should also know everyone on their children's friends list—just as we'd want to know who they're hanging out with in person.

MySpace Doesn't Always Look or Act Like We Say It Will

MySpace may not always behave or look exactly the way we describe in this chapter. There are two reasons for this. One, of course, is that MySpace changes things; that's the nature of the Web. But the more likely reason—especially when you're visiting profiles of teenagers or young adults—is that MySpace is extremely customisable, so its users can really play with anonymity.

MySpace provides lots of ways to radically alter the appearance of a page, including changing the fonts and colours, and even removing or moving standard elements that are there by default (we cover this in Chapter 7). So if we tell you to click a box and you can't find it, it's not because you (or we) are getting senile. It's because the owner of that profile has done a "hack" to change things around (you'll find more on hacking in Chapter 7). Usually, if you look hard enough, you will find things like the person's Contacting box, but it may not look familiar at all.

Using MySpace Mail

Mail is your central MySpace communication tool. This email-like interface lives on your MySpace home page and lets you contact a user, receive notifications, and hear from friends and other MySpace users.

Unlike your usual email, MySpace mail is internal to the service. It's used by fellow MySpace users to communicate with one another and is not designed to send and receive messages across the Internet to users of other email services. By default, MySpace does send messages to your usual email account (your login email address), notifying you that you have mail, comments, blog posts, invitations, and so on waiting in your MySpace account. You can turn those notifications off in Account Settings if you want.

Whenever you log into MySpace, new mail messages are flagged in bold red in your My Mail box on the left side of your home page.

To read mail messages, follow these steps.

1. In the My Mail box on your home page, click the red New Messages! link or the Inbox link (**FIGURE 4.7**).

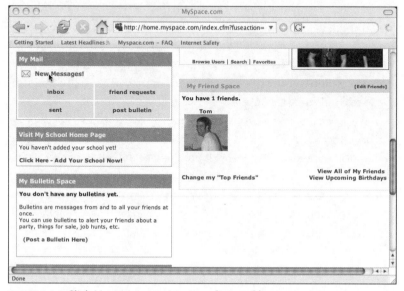

FIGURE 4.7 Click New Messages! to see what mail has come in.

2. Open the message by clicking the subject link.

3. Use the buttons at the bottom of the message screen to reply to the message or delete it.

Don't ask us why, but you don't send messages from your MySpace mail or even from your home page. To send a message, follow these steps.

1. On the profile page of the friend you want to contact, click Send Message in the Contacting box.

   A blank mail-message window, addressed to that user, opens (**FIGURE 4.8**).

   Remember, it's possible that the person may have *hacked*, or altered, the page, and you won't see or you might have trouble recognising the Contacting box. Before you give up on contacting the person, look around carefully; the Contacting box with its

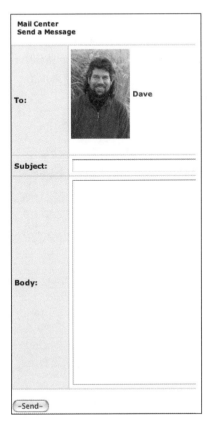

Mail Center
Send a Message

To: Dave

Subject:

Body:

-Send-

FIGURE 4.8 The message window,
where you type your email.

eight links (Send Message, Add to Friends, Instant Message, etc.) is
probably still there. Even people who love spiffing up their profiles
still want to receive messages from friends.

2. Type your message in the Body text box.

3. Click Send.

Sent messages are stored in the Sent box for 14 days, and you can
check their status (whether the messages were sent, read, or replied to).
Currently, this feature is a privacy issue, in that it makes spying easier:
You can tell whether a user has read your message, and others can do the
same when they view messages they've sent you recently. At the moment,
Account Privacy Settings don't address this issue.

KEY PARENTING POINT

Young users are likely to get mail from people they don't know. As with all email, they should be careful about responding or clicking links in those messages that could take them to inappropriate websites, and they should be careful about responding to any offers that come via email.

Using the Address Book

MySpace offers an address book that lets you store information about your friends and other contacts.

To begin managing your address book, follow these steps.

1. Click the Manage Address Book link in the Hello box on your home page.

2. Use the Quick Add Contact feature to start building your address book (**FIGURE 4.9**).

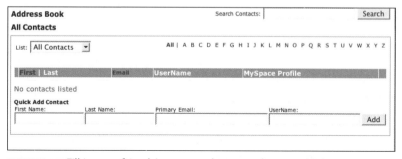

FIGURE 4.9 Fill in your friends' names and contact data to add them to your address book.

Populate the name, email, and user-name fields, and click Add. If you enter just the email address, the address book will populate the UserName field and MySpace page details field automatically.

3. You can add more information at any time by clicking the View a Contact link and then clicking Edit at the bottom of the screen (**FIGURE 4.10**).

FIGURE 4.10 Edit your friends' contact info on the View a Contact page.

Using Bulletins

Bulletins are an easy way to contact or send news to several MySpace friends all at once.

To post a bulletin, follow these steps.

1. In My Mail (on your home page), click Post Bulletin. The Post Bulletin page appears.

2. Enter a Subject line, and write your message in the Body text box.

3. Click the Post button at the bottom of the page. A confirmation screen appears.

4. Verify the posting, edit it, or cancel it (**FIGURE 4.11**).

FIGURE 4.11 Confirm that you want to send this message to all your friends.

<u>KEY PARENTING POINT</u>

Mass bulletin posts are fairly common in MySpace culture. What MySpace users should remember—particularly those with numerous friends—is that these posts go out to everyone. For privacy and self-protection, remind children not to reveal personal information, such as their email address, phone number, home address, or where they plan to hang out that night. It's also thoughtful to avoid spamming friends with too many messages.

Reading Bulletins

Because of the frequency of bulletin posts, MySpace doesn't notify users when a new one has been posted, unlike mail messages, comments, and new invites.

To check the latest bulletin posts, go to the My Bulletin Space on your MySpace home page. Bulletins are listed sequentially, starting with the most current posting.

To open and read a message, click the subject link in the Bulletin column (**FIGURE 4.12**).

Blocking Bulletins

Bulletins are great communication tools, but they can easily become annoying and spamlike. If you are receiving unwanted or excessive bulletins, the only way to block them is to delete the sender as a friend. To do this, open the bulletin, and click the Delete from Friends button on the bottom-right side of the screen.

Modifying Your Top 8

On MySpace, "Your Top 8" refers to the featured friends in your My Friend Space on your profile page. When you first join MySpace and start building your network, the first eight friends will automatically populate this window. As you make more friends, you can opt to prioritise who is in your Top 8.

FIGURE 4.12 Click the subject link in the Bulletin column to read that message.

What this means varies from user to user. Some MySpace fans might feature all their top MySpace friends—those who actively socialise and participate online. Others might prioritise, based on their real-world friends, regardless of whether they are big MySpace users. Others try to balance all the key people in their life and evenly cover friends, family, and colleagues—or be really safe and top the list with their girlfriend, boyfriend, and siblings, and then be diplomatic and fill the rest of the slots with bands representing their favourite music. A workaround some MySpace users employ is to hack their profile to feature their "Top 20" or "Top 30" instead, or even to hide this section altogether. (For details about how to do this, see Chapter 7.)

In any case, the Top 8 list is very visible and can be a social minefield if not given much thought. Youngsters are usually very mindful of this, but the question of how they rank people on this list or how much they think about it could be an interesting parent-child talking point or even a teachable moment.

Deleting Friends

You can delete existing friends at any time by following these steps.

1. In the Friend area of your home page, click the Edit Friends link in
    the top-right corner (**FIGURE 4.13**).

FIGURE 4.13 Click Edit Friends to update your friends. (It does help to have
more than one friend!)

2. On the Edit Friends page, check the box beside the photo of the
    friend you want to delete.
3. Click Delete Selected to delete that friend.

Friends whom you delete will *not* be notified about the deletion,
though they will probably figure it out when you no longer appear as
their friend.

Commenting on Other People's Profiles

Comments are in many ways the social glue of MySpace, and they provide
a quick, fun, and popular way for online users to connect and stay in touch.
As anyone who's visited a hall of residence knows, students like to put
things on each other's doors, and MySpace lets users do just that.

Unlike more private emails, these bulletin-board-like posts allow friends
to publicly share thoughts, expressions, plans, and more—which means at
times that people can learn a lot about your children's personal business.

Plus when someone posts a comment, it kind of reflects on the person whose page it's on.

We urge MySpace users who allow others to post comments to check their profiles often (if they don't already!) to make sure no one posted anything that invades their privacy, or is embarrassing or otherwise inappropriate. It's also a good idea to check friends' profiles to see whether and where comments about you show up.

Profile Comments

These comments are the most public of MySpace features, appearing as they do right on your main profile page.

You must be someone's friend to post a comment on his or her profile, and users can set Privacy Settings to require approval before posting (see Chapter 3 for more details). But if you have a public profile, almost anyone can view your profile and its comments, should he or she come across it.

To post a comment in a friend's profile.

1. On your friend's profile page, scroll to the bottom of the Friends Comments section, and click Add Comment (**FIGURE 4.14**).

2. Type your comment in the text box.

3. Click Submit.

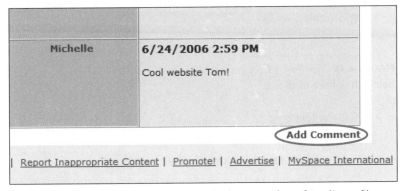

Michelle	**6/24/2006 2:59 PM**
	Cool website Tom!
	Add Comment
Report Inappropriate Content	Promote!	Advertise	MySpace International

FIGURE 4.14 You can add a comment at the bottom of any friend's profile.

Picture Comments

MySpace picture galleries are another spot where you can share your thoughts and hellos. Users are allowed to upload a maximum of eight photos and images to their profile, and friends often like to comment on pics that catch their attention.

To add a picture comment, do the following.

1. On your friend's profile page, click the Pics link below the profile picture.

2. In the picture gallery, click the picture you want to comment on.

3. Click Post a Comment below the photo (**FIGURE 4.15**).

Larry as a baby

» **Post A Comment**
» **Report This Image**

0 Comment(s)

FIGURE 4.15 Click Post a Comment below the photo of choice.

4. Fill in the text box.

   A Confirm Comment screen will pop up.

5. Click Post Comment to publish the comment.

   If your friend has turned on commenting privacy, you will have to wait until your friend approves the comment before it displays.

Commenting and Privacy

To best protect your online self and reputation from potential unwanted comments and posts, you may want to consider enabling the Approve Comments Before Posting feature in the Privacy Settings section of your Account Settings.

This feature will allow you to review and approve all comments before anyone can see them. You'll be notified via email, and the user will receive a message, after they've posted a comment, saying you must approve their post first.

To activate this feature, follow these steps.

1. On your MySpace home page, click Account Settings and then click the red Change Settings link beside Privacy Settings.

2. Scroll down to My Privacy Settings, and check Approve Comments Before Posting (**FIGURE 4.16**).

3. Click Change Settings.

My Privacy Settings	
☐	Require email or last name to add me as a friend
☑	Approve Comments before Posting
☐	Hide Online Now
☐	Show My Birthday to my Friends 🎂
☐	No Pic Forwarding
☐	Friend Only Blog Comments
☐	Block Friend Request From Bands
☐	Friend Only Group Invites
☐	Disable Band Songs From Automatically Starting
Who Can View My Full Profile	
○	My Friends Only
◉	Public
Change Settings Cancel	

FIGURE 4.16 People can say anything they want in *your* profile unless you check Approve Comments Before Posting in your Privacy Settings.

Editing and Deleting Comments

Although only friends can write comments in users' profiles, blogs, and photos, there is always the possibility that someone will post something that's undesirable, embarrassing, inappropriate, or jeopardises your privacy. That's why users have the ability to delete comments that others put on their profiles.

If someone posts a comment you don't approve of, you can easily delete the posting.

To delete profile comments, follow these steps.

1. Under your picture in your Hello Box, click Profile.

2. Scroll to the Comments section of your profile and click View/Edit All (**FIGURE 4.17**).

3. Find the comment you wish to delete and click Delete Comment.

4. When MySpace asks you to confirm, click OK.

To delete unwanted comments people have posted about a photo or image you've posted in your profile, do the following.

1. On your home page, click Profile in the Hello box to display a page containing all your uploaded pictures.

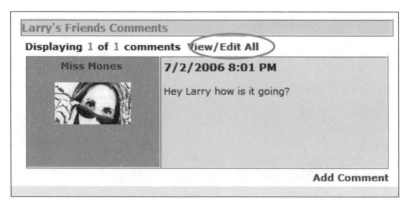

FIGURE 4.17 You can delete comments by clicking View/Edit All in the comments area of your profile.

2. To view and edit comments, click the applicable picture.
    The photo will appear with the comment next to it.

3. Click Delete to remove the comment.

TIP

If your Profile Settings are HTML-enabled, people can post pictures and images, as well as text comments. To delete these types of "comments," follow the steps in the previous list.

MySpace Events

MySpace Event Invites are other pieces of MySpace mail that may pop up in your or your child's Inbox quite often. (Some bands and other groups send Invites to huge swathes of MySpace users.) These invitations might announce shows, concerts, or parties coming up—or friends may be forwarding you the invites they get.

To view Event Invites at any time, take these steps.

1. Click the Events tab on the blue navigational bar of any page.

2. Click the Event Invites link on the left side of the screen.

You can also find Event Invites in your regular MySpace inbox.

TIP

You can't turn off receiving these invites in your MySpace mail, but you can change your account settings so you don't get them in your usual (non-MySpace) email account. You can do this from Account Settings (in the Hello box on your home page) by checking the Do Not Send Me Notification Emails box, located beside Notifications.

To send an event invitation, use this process.

1. Click MySpace Events on the blue navigation bar of any page.

2. Click Create New Event.

3. Fill in the applicable fields, and click Invite & Update (**FIGURE 4.18**).

FIGURE 4.18 Fill in the message box and the email addresses of the people you want to invite.

4. On the next screen, you can opt to include a personal message, show the guest list to everyone, ask invitees to RSVP, import emails from the Hotmail or Yahoo! accounts of people you want to invite, or invite MySpace users.

5. Click Invite and then click Update.

Photo Rankings

For better or worse, the Photo Rankings feature lets you rate the attractiveness or coolness of other people's photos. You or your child can choose to submit them—or not. Ranking is on a scale of 1 to 10.

Adding your image to the rating system will allow other users to view and rate your image. Keep in mind that a person does not need to be your friend to comment.

To submit a photo for ranking, do the following.

1. On your MySpace home page, click Add/Edit Photos.

2. Select the photo you want to submit, and click the Add to Ranking button directly below it (**FIGURE 4.19**).

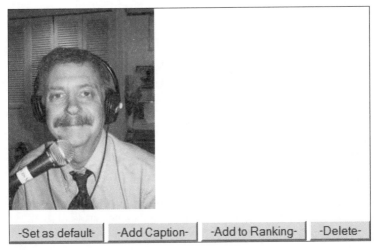

| -Set as default- | -Add Caption- | -Add to Ranking- | -Delete- |

FIGURE 4.19 Select the photo you want ranked and click the Add to Ranking button.

To see what people think about your pic, go to your MySpace home page, and click the Ranking Score button.

Your Ranking Score is private and for your eyes only, though as mentioned earlier in this chapter, if you submit a picture, anyone can rank it.

To rank a MySpacer's picture, follow these steps.

1. Visit the user's profile, and click the Rank User link in the Contacting box.

    If the user has submitted a photo for ranking, you'll be taken to a window displaying the photo, as well as a ranking scale.

2. To vote, simply click the applicable number (**FIGURE 4.20**).

    If the MySpace user hasn't submitted a photo for ranking, you'll get a screen telling you this and suggesting that you contact them.

FIGURE 4.20 Submit your photo, and people can rate you on a page like this. Some people aspire to be in MySpace's Top 25 (among 80 million-plus!)

KEY PARENTING POINT

MySpace isn't the first site to include photo ratings. A lot of teenagers go to RateMe.com or HotorNot.com, among many other sites to submit their photos and be rated. While some people might enjoy positive rankings, others could wind up feeling humiliated. Talk with your son or daughter about whether or not you think it's a good idea to submit pictures for ranking and how you feel about them rating other people's pictures.

MySpace Communities

MySpace is all about "communities," be they a group of friends from the same city or school; people who have a common lifestyle, religion, or political viewpoint; or people who gather together around broader communities such as music, films, books, or a particular band, genre, author, or film. In other words, a community is anything that two or more people say it is.

Some communities are strictly virtual—most of the members probably have never met face to face—and others are an extension of real-life communities, such as those built around a particular school, hobby, sports team, or workplace.

We can't possibly write about even a fraction of the communities that have formed through the service, but we can talk about some of MySpace's major interest areas. The other thing we can't do is to point you to one screen or menu that lists all the communities, but we can help you find your way around.

Finding Community

One place to look for community is in the main navigation bar at the top of every page. There, you'll find links to Film, Videos, and Music. You'll also find links to Blog, which is where some people find community (in a more text-based way), and Groups, which is the natural spot for people gathering around specific topics.

Another place to look is the pale-blue box below the navigation bar on MySpace's home page (to get there, click the MySpace.com link at the top of any page). In that box, you'll find the many communities MySpace has added more recently: Comedy, Filmmakers, Games, Horoscopes, Movies, Music Videos, and Schools. That same box will take you to communities built around specific community tools: Blogs, MySpaceIM, Chat Rooms, and Groups (**FIGURE 4.21**).

All in all, community on MySpace is pretty much wherever you are.

Music

Music—and promoting independent musicians—has always been an integral part of MySpace. Music is the leading MySpace community and home to thousands of artists of every genre, from garage bands and indies to major recording artists, who have profiles complete with songs, biogs, lyrics, and more (**FIGURE 4.22**). You'll find a link to the Music community on the blue navigation bar near the top of every page.

FIGURE 4.21 To get a feel for the sheer number and diversity of MySpace Groups, glance through the 222,683 groups under Music alone. (Music is the original MySpace interest group.)

FIGURE 4.22 MySpace Music's home page.

Founded as a platform for independent and startup artists to help them gain more exposure, this part of MySpace has become such a force and fan base that mainstream musicians are now participating as well, including Madonna, Shakira, and Keith Urban.

Each country has different musical tastes, and which music site you see depends on where you are logged in from, so your teenagers will find that MySpace gives them the local bands they want to listen to and not just US music.

Music profiles work pretty much the same as other MySpace pages with a slight change in look and feel. Musicians can upload as many as three songs to their profiles; other MySpacers can choose to add these songs to their profiles as a personalisation feature.

Film

Film is also a link on the main blue navigation bar. The Film community is a portal for independent filmmakers to gain exposure, to network and build fan bases, and to showcase their work. The functionality parallels that of MySpace Music and has features for indie filmmakers and fans, including a search function to locate filmmakers by role, location, film, or keyword; a list of top filmmakers by genre; and a list of screenings in your area.

You'll also find filmmaker forums, where the artists answer questions and discuss their films with fans. And just in case you or your teenager wants to make it big on the big screen, there's a classified section with listings for industry jobs, auditions, casting calls, and more.

Books

There's a link to Books in the box just below the navigation bar on the MySpace.com home page. This section features book reviews, blogs, and featured book groups, as well as a Top Books section and search functionality. It's like an ordinary book group, only virtual, and with lots more information, but no tea and biscuits (**FIGURE 4.23**).

FIGURE 4.23 Your 24/7 virtual book group.

Comedy

You'll find a link to Comedy in the same box as Books. The section has a variety of humour-related content and interaction. Similar to the Music and Film portals, MySpace Comedy is a platform for comedians to gain exposure, network, and build a fan base, as well as another venue where users (and aspiring professional comics) can socialise although unlike music it is US-specific.

Comedians can post profiles, list and search for gigs, and network in the forum. MySpacers can peruse forums and exchange jokes and funny stories; search for sketches, improv, and stand-up comedy shows; and check out the week's funniest MySpace video (**FIGURE 4.24**).

KEY PARENTING POINT

Hard as it is to imagine a comedian telling a dirty joke, there can be off-colour comedy here that some parents may feel is inappropriate for teenagers. We recommend that you check out this forum firsthand and gauge whether or not you feel comfortable with your child's perusing the material.

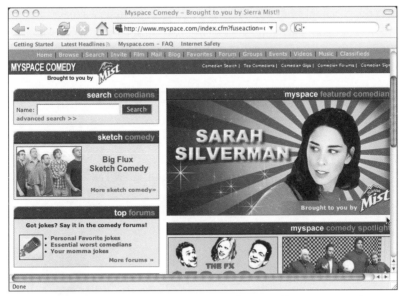

FIGURE 4.24 For MySpacers seeking a little comic relief (or serious professional networking), check out the Comedy section.

Games

MySpace (or any cross-section of online life) would be incomplete without a section devoted to video, online, and PC games. This type of interactive entertainment is a big part of virtual communities and social networking, and several classic multiplayer games (such as Dungeons & Dragons) have helped spawn modern online social networks. MySpace Categories include sports, action, trivia, card games like solitaire, board games, and puzzles.

Games is basically a portal where gamers can connect, play solo, and compete with other MySpace users.

Schools

The MySpace Schools community is a sort of after-school virtual hangout for secondary school and university students and alumni, but its biggest and most vocal group is clearly secondary school students. University students are more likely to hang out on Facebook (more on that in a moment). In case you missed it, in Chapter 2 we talked about how secondary school students use MySpace and, as we hope we made clear, it is a vast network of communities of students most commonly socialising with friends at their own schools (**FIGURE 4.25**).

FIGURE 4.25 Each of the Top 10 schools has more than 1,000 MySpace members!

Finding Classmates

A lot of children use MySpace's search feature to find classmates from their school. Here's how.

1. On the main blue navigation bar near the top of any page, click Search.

2. In the Find Your Classmates section, type the school name, and select your country from the pulldown menu. Region/County will be greyed out for UK searches.

3. Click Find.

    A list of schools that meet your search requirements appears.

4. Click the name of the school to start your search.

You can narrow your search by gender; age range (starting with 16); marital status; dating status; whether they're current students or alumni; year of graduation; and even more options.

Although this feature is primarily used by current students, Larry tried it out on his high-school graduating class of "a long time ago." Out of about a thousand people from his class, he found three classmates.

Locating School Groups

Schools have always been a powerful source of community, and so it is on the social-networking scene. If you have a school in your present or past, MySpace aims to have a forum for you, the service tells us.

Each school forum (also called a group) has its own moderator, who applies to MySpace for the job. "We personally review each school-moderator application form," a spokesperson from MySpace told us. The moderator's job is to keep the discussion appropriate and on topic (he or she can block users and delete posts). Classmates can also rate the moderator, and MySpace reviews those ratings; enough negative ones can get the moderator replaced (MySpace staff stay in touch with school moderators).

School forums have their own classified ads associated with them, so users can swap or sell textbooks, find bands for leavers' balls, or hire a tutor. MySpace distinguishes between secondary-school classifieds (which don't include ads for roommates and accommodation) and university-level ones (which do). Both current students and alumni are welcome in the school forums.

If you want to locate your child's or any school group on MySpace, here's how.

1. Click Groups on the main navigation bar and then click Search Groups in the little blue box on the left.
2. In the Groups Advanced Search window, type the school's name.
3. Choose Schools & Alumni from the Category pulldown menu.
4. For some countries, though not the UK, choose the school's state from the State pulldown menu.
5. To narrow your search further, select a choice in the Miles From pull-down menu and fill in the post code in the Post Code box (**FIGURE 4.26**).

Groups that match your search are displayed. These could include a group of current students, an alumni group, the Class of 2002, or any other group associated with that school (**FIGURE 4.27**).

FIGURE 4.26 Type your school name and location information and make a choice from the Schools & Alumni category to find all the forums associated with your school.

FIGURE 4.27 Here are some of the forums associated with Warwick School (among other schools around the country).

TIP

We found that you really need to type the school's post code and choose a number from the Miles From pulldown menu (the Any option doesn't work) to zoom in on your school of choice.

Facebook: The 'Other' Student Social-Networking Site

Although MySpace is certainly used by plenty of university students, another social-networking site, called Facebook, is very popular in higher education (**FIGURE 4.28**). Facebook started off as a site for US undergraduates but is now open to everyone and has an extensive UK presence.

FIGURE 4.28 The very spare Facebook home page.

When Facebook started it was only available to college students who had to use their university-provided email address (ending in .edu) to register. Gradually the limitations on who could register were relaxed, and in Autumn 2006 Facebook was opened up to anyone who wanted to join.

This might make it less popular with the students who were there originally, as one of the main things people seemed to like about it was that you knew you were making friends with fellow students of about the same age.

Chat Rooms

A *chat room* is an online space where people "chat" by typing and sending short messages to people on the same page in real time. Entering a chat room is essentially the virtual equivalent of a cocktail party. You schmooze, socialise, *maybe* connect, and have extended conversations with one or more individuals, but in-depth conversations are rare, to say the least.

Because MySpace is a social network, chat rooms are a popular feature. There are numerous chat rooms in MySpace Chat, organised by categories and topics.

To log on to a chat room, do the following.

1. Go to the main MySpace home page by clicking the MySpace.com link (top-left corner of any page).

2. Click the Chat Rooms link in the pale-blue box just below the main navigational bar.

   You'll see three tabs, with options to search by categories, location, or age (**FIGURE 4.29**).

FIGURE 4.29 There are numerous chat rooms in MySpace Chat, organised by categories and topics, from Food & Drink to Television to Business & Money.

3. Click the desired tab and then a subtopic on that tab.

   You'll be logged into the applicable chat room automatically.

4. To start a conversation or announce your presence, type a short message in the text box on the bottom-right side of the page (next to Style) and then press the return key or click the Send button (**FIGURE 4.30**).

5. To leave a chat room at any time, just close the application window by clicking the X (located on the top right on Windows screens and top left on Macintosh screens).

KEY PARENTING POINT

MySpace does have moderators who, from time to time, check the chat rooms for disruptive and inappropriate behaviour, but they're not working around the clock, and they're not in every chat room. Even if they're there, moderators can deal with problems only after the fact. So children need to know what not to say and to be on the lookout for rude, obnoxious, and occasionally dangerous people.

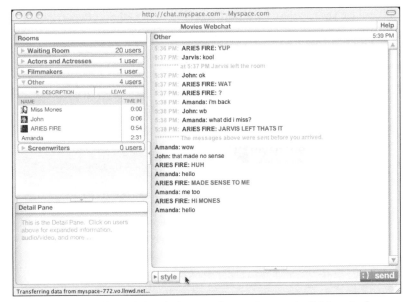

FIGURE 4.30 Each line of chat (a few words at a time, typically) is a single person's comment or response; the dialogue is usually very casual.

When you enter the room, you'll see streams of short messages among the visitors. You can read the threads and get the gist of what's going on or dive right in. Lots of people *lurk,* watching the conversation for a bit before jumping in. Typical online etiquette is to announce your presence with something like "Hi, people."

MySpace has age-related chat rooms for teenagers and people in their 20s, 30s, and so on. Having a space just for younger users is a terrific idea—and the room is off limits to anyone whose stated age is older than 20—but there is nothing to stop older people from going into that room by lying about their age. There is also nothing to stop teenagers from entering rooms for older users, even if they don't lie about their age.

Although there are moderators for some chat rooms, moderators don't patrol the rooms 100 per cent of the time. We recommend that if at any time you notice disruptive or inappropriate behaviour, you should just leave the chat room. To leave, simply close the application window. If you notice that some user is repeatedly causing a disturbance, and a moderator isn't intervening, you can file a complaint or report the user to MySpace Customer Care by clicking the Contact MySpace link at the bottom of every page (choose Report Abuse below Please Select a Topic in the Contact Request box).

KEY PARENTING POINT

Chat is not a great place for children anywhere on the Internet, unless it's clearly designated for children only and monitored 24/7 by responsible human beings (AOL's Kids Only is one example). This is because conversations in chat rooms can easily and quickly become sexually explicit. And tempers can flare in chat rooms; people can forget their manners (kind of like the way some people act when they're angry while driving a car). When your children are in a chat room, what they type can be seen immediately by everyone else in the room; there's no way to take it back. So warn them to be careful not to enter anything that personally identifies them or that they might later regret having said.

Let your children know that if they see something that's hurtful, they should try not to take it personally; it says more about the person saying it than about them. In general, MySpace profiles and blogs, where users have some editing control and are generally "talking" with their friends, are better for teenagers.

Forums

Forums are for holding discussions online and are great resources for questions, help, and advice. On other sites, they are commonly referred to as message boards, discussion boards, and bulletin boards.

Forums differ from chat rooms and instant messaging because they focus more on single topics, are generally more in-depth than chat, and don't encourage real-time personal interaction. Still, you need to be careful that you don't say anything inappropriate and have a thick skin in case someone else forgets to mind their manners.

To participate in MySpace Forums, take these steps.

1. Click Forum on the blue navigational bar at the top of any MySpace screen.

    On the Forum home page, you'll see folders or categories with short descriptions (**FIGURE 4.31**).

2. Click the desired topic and scroll through the listed subtopics until you see one of interest.

| Home | Browse | Search | Invite | Film | Mail | Blog | Favorites | Forum | Groups |

Forum Home

Forum Category	Rooms	Topics	Posts
Automotive Talk about your ride. We did it for TheBoz.	Chat	25457	509751
Business & Entrepreneurs Need advice or a partner for your latest venture?	Chat	11288	43000
Campus Life Study partners, PARTIES, and alumni.	Chat	9450	58895
Career Center Career advice, discussion and opportunities.	Chat	7640	30910
Comedy Forums for comics and lovers of comedy.	Chat	1650	17686
Computers & Technology From PCs to iPods; technoid congregation.	Chat	20720	158628
Culture, Arts & Literature The finer things in life be here.	Chat	12566	116582

FIGURE 4.31 There are many topics and subtopics to choose among in these folders. (You'll note that there's chat on these subjects, too, but people usually don't stay on topic in chat.)

3. To post a topic, click Post a Topic (top-right corner), enter a subject, type your question or comment, and click Post This Topic.

     You'll see a Preview Topic confirmation screen.

4. Click Post This Topic to publish your comment.

5. Check back regularly to see how other MySpacers have responded to your post.

KEY PARENTING POINT

As we mention elsewhere in the book, we run a parents' forum about social-networking safety at BlogSafety.com. It's a great way to test out this technology and maybe pick up some tips from other parents in the process.

Instant Messaging

MySpace introduced an instant-messaging feature in June 2006 very similar to the popular AIM (AOL Instant Messaging) and Yahoo! and MSN (Microsoft) Messenger services (**FIGURE 4.32**). Unlike other aspects of MySpace that work within your Web browser, to use this service, you must download a separate piece of software. As of this writing, the MySpaceIM service works only with Windows (sorry, Mac users).

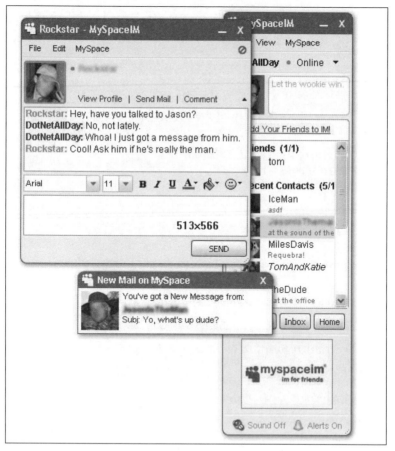

FIGURE 4.32 MySpaceIM works a lot like other instant-messaging services, so it'll be very easy for your children to pick up (if they haven't already!)

To download the MySpaceIM program, do the following.

1. On the MySpace.com home page (not *your* home page), click MySpaceIM in the box just below the main toolbar.

2. Click the Download MySpaceIM link, which downloads an installation program that you can run to install the software.

Pay close attention to messages from your browser. You may have to select a security option to allow a download.

When the MySpaceIM software is installed, run the program, and fill in your email address and MySpace password just as you do when you sign into MySpace. The software can be configured to remember this information in the future.

Before you can start exchanging messages with friends, you have to add them to IM by clicking Add Your Friends to IM! just below your photo. You'll see a list of your friends, whom you can add by clicking their profile names.

Then, when you're signed on, you'll see a list of your friends who are online and also running the IM software. To send someone an instant message, double-click his or her name, and you get to a box where you can start typing your message.

KEY PARENTING POINT

Unless we use IM at work, most teenagers know more about instant messaging than we'll ever know, and even if we're fluent, they use it differently than we do—with multiple conversations and other tasks running simultaneously. It's tough to get a word in, but if you can, try to get your kids to include only people they know personally in their IM friends lists—and to remember that people can copy and paste their comments elsewhere, beyond their control. They need to think before they post here, too.

There are some optional privacy features in MySpaceIM, which you can configure by choosing File > Preferences in the IM program and then clicking Privacy. Your choices allow you to be contacted by anyone or only people in your contact list (we recommend the latter, of course). You can also list specific people you want to block from contacting you.

While you're looking at Preferences, check out General Preferences, which give you control over what picture to display in IM, as well as control over some other features.

Also look at the Appearance options, which control how the IM program looks, and the Contact List options, which help you manage your contact list. You can also change the alerts and sound, which is a very good idea if you're using IM in an office or classroom, where you don't want others to hear sounds when you send and receive messages.

Blogging

This area of MySpace can be a bit confusing because, technically speaking, all of MySpace is a kind of feature-rich blogging tool. But the way the company handles blogs is to treat them as a separate feature. MySpace was one of the first social networks to make profiles the central focus. Blogs are optional, and from what we've seen, most children don't bother with them, opting instead to use their profiles to keep up with their friends.

Blogs are more for people who are into written expression. Still, parents should be aware of blogging, because many young people do use it when they feel like being the host of an ongoing discussion (slightly more substantive, sometimes, than profile comments) or having their very own platform for sharing insights, writing, artwork, and more.

To set up a MySpace blog, do the following.

1. Click Manage Blog in the Hello box on your MySpace home page.

2. In the My Controls area on the left side of the page, select Post New Blog (**FIGURE 4.33**).

   The phrase *Post New Blog* can be misleading, especially to anyone who's worked with other blogs. You're not necessarily creating a new blog. What this option really means is that you're creating a new blog posting or entry.

3. Enter the requested information.

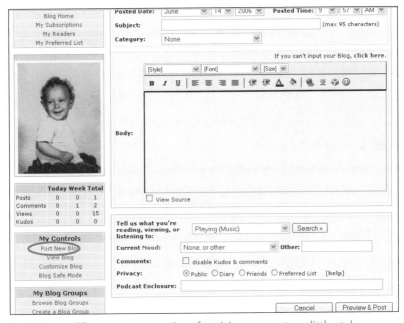

FIGURE 4.33 There are many options for giving your entry a little style.

4. Type your post in the Body section (or paste text from your word processor).

5. Add anything else you want, such as music and current mood.

6. Decide whether you want to allow people to comment and who you want to view the blog.

7. Click Preview & Post in the bottom-right corner.

You'll be able to preview what you've created before you actually post.

Blog Privacy

At the bottom of the Post a New Blog Entry screen is a place where you can designate whether each new entry is Public (readable by anyone), Diary (readable only by you), Friends (for your friends only), or Preferred List (which makes it available only to people you put on that list).

On the blog-entry page, you can also specify who is on your preferred list by clicking My Preferred List near the top-left side of the page, just above your photo. That same area has menu items that allow you to view who subscribes to your blog and to manage your subscriptions to other blogs.

You also can choose the Disable Kudos and Comments option so that others can't post items on your blog.

Blog Comments

If you have friends who regularly post to their blogs, you might occasionally read one and want to respond, start a discussion, or connect in some way.

To post a comment, you need to do the following.

1. Scroll to the bottom of your friend's blog, and click Add Comment.

2. In the text box, write your message.

3. Click Post.

To delete unwanted blog comments, simply take these steps.

1. Click View My Blog on your MySpace home page.

2. Select the offending comment.

3. Click the Remove link below it (**FIGURE 4.34**).

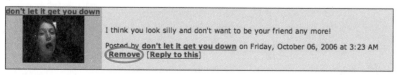

FIG 4.34 Click the Remove link to delete a blog posting.

Blog Safe Mode

Listed under My Controls on your blog home page, Blog Safe mode allows you to view your HTML code in a blog without affecting formatting, so you can fix any problems. Because you need to know a bit of HTML to use it, this mode is really designed for advanced users. It's certainly not rocket science, but it is a more advanced feature that many users don't use. You can learn more about HTML in Chapter 7.

Tackling Safety Issues

By now, you're a MySpace "expert," at least compared with most parents. Knowing the basics of how to use the service is a great start. But now it's time to take your hands off the keyboard and start thinking about hands-on parenting in the digital age. In the next chapter, we talk about safety, but before you run and hide, at least read the first few pages. You might be pleased to learn that it's not quite as dangerous out there as some people might have you believe.

CHAPTER 5

Social Networking Safely

BASED ON RECENT NEWS REPORTS, you might think that
something incredibly dangerous has burst on the scene—that
there's a predator lurking behind nearly every keyboard
waiting to sexually assault a teenager. Well, predators and
tragic cases of sexual assault do exist, but before you yank
the broadband modem out of the wall, consider the
real risks.

We recently heard about a video that exposes the
"current pandemic of sexual predation via the Internet"
(from a company that offers a monitoring service), and
plenty of other people are only too willing to tell you about
the "growing epidemic" of children who have been victims
of Internet-related sexual exploitation. It's enough to scare
a parent to death.

But despite a handful of truly tragic situations, the facts are that:

- the odds of your child being the victim of Internet-related sexual violence are extremely low
- there are much more likely risks that the headlines often overlook.

Most news reports about MySpace in the first few months of 2006 concerned a handful of tragic cases involving men contacting teenage girls on MySpace and persuading them to meet offline for sex. Then the number of school-related stories about threats to peers and teachers started growing.

We've also seen a few stories about identity theft on MySpace. Most of these stories concerned childrens' user names and passwords—in other words, the peer-to-peer harassment we'll be hearing more about from the media as reporters move beyond the predation story.

First, the Research

Though statistics about risks in social-networking sites haven't been compiled, we do know some things about sexual predation online.

It's Usually Not 'Stranger Danger'

A US study published in 1994 by the University of New Hampshire (UNH) Crimes Against Children Research Center, the main source of data on child exploitation, concluded that 70 per cent to 90 per cent of sexual abuse is committed by "persons known to the child." When the victim has been a girl, a third to a half of the crimes are committed by family members. When the victim has been a boy, 10 per cent to 20 per cent of the perpetrators are family members.

Detective Frank Dannahey is the youth officer in the Police Department of the town of Rocky Hill, Connecticut. He told us that most of the sexual-assault cases he works on involve people the victims know.
"I think probably the number of reports about MySpace we see in the media isn't an accurate representation of what really happens." Still, he feels young people need to understand the potential.

Dannahey appeared on the US TV show "Dateline NBC" in April 2006 to illustrate how "stranger danger" can occur when teenage girls allow themselves to be deceived by a clever adult (in this case, himself) using a MySpace profile to pose as a teenage boy (see page 114).

Deception Is Not the Norm

Many people believe that online sexual predators are usually older men posing as teenagers, but research suggests that's not the case. Another study published by UNH in 2004—this time about *Net*-related sexual-exploitation crimes against minors—found that only 5 per cent of offenders tried to deceive victims about being older adults; only 21 per cent misrepresented their sexual motives, and most of those deceptions involved promises of love and romance, not the offender's ultimate objective.

Force Is Seldom Used

The 2004 study also found that only 5 per cent of offenders used force, 16 per cent used coercion, and 3 per cent used abduction to sexually exploit their victims. This suggests that, in most cases where young people are victimised, the exploitation is consensual. The research also suggests that it may be misleading to categorise offenders in such cases as strangers, because victims and offenders had typically communicated, both online and by telephone, for more than one month prior to meeting in person.

Young Teenagers Are More Vulnerable

The 2004 study also found that 76 per cent of the victims were between 13 and 15 years old, that 1 per cent were 12 years old, and that no victim was younger than 12.

As for child exploitation in general, the number of reported cases of sexual assaults against children has actually gone down precisely during the time when Internet use among young people has exploded. On August 8, 2005, *USA Today* reporter Wendy Koch cited government figures showing that "the rate of sexual assaults against adolescents ages 12 to 17 plunged 79% from 1993 through 2003, and the number of substantiated sex-abuse cases involving kids of all ages fell 39% in the same time period" (**FIGURE 5.1**).

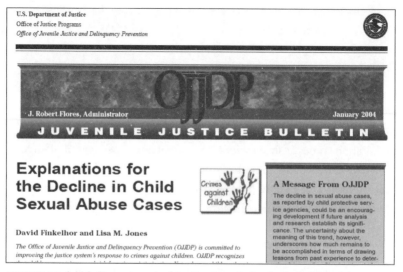

FIGURE 5.1 A U.S. Department of Justice *Juvenile Justice Bulletin* explains reasons for the decline in child sexual abuse cases.

So far, virtually all the data about Internet sexual crimes against children come from studies done before the founding of MySpace and other social-networking services, but in terms of risk factors, researchers have told us that social networking is not much different from email, instant messaging (IM), and other online communication tools.

What we do know is that the number of actual sexual-exploitation cases is small relative to the millions of young people who use these sites. Let's take a hard look at the data.

Interpreting the Numbers

On July 3rd 2006 the *Daily Mail* warned its readers that there had been a
"Paedophile warning over teen websites bebo and MySpace." The warning
came from the headmistress of a girls' grammar school in Tunbridge Wells
in Kent who had expressed alarm over the discovery that 700 of her pupils
had signed up to the sites, and some had posted personal information and
revealing pictures.

FIGURE 5.2 The *Daily Mail* is keen to warn its readers of the dangers of
MySpace and other teen websites.

It was just one of many stories about the dangers of online predators
targetting children who use social networking sites. These stories have
been around for years, long before MySpace was invented. In 2001 Carol
Vorderman appeared on *Tonight with Trevor McDonald* on ITV to alert
parents to the dangers of grooming, and since then radio, television and
both tabloid and broadsheet newspapers have followed suit.

The dangers are certainly real, as we saw in April 2006 when 21-year-
old student Lee Costi was jailed for 9 years after he had sex with two

girls aged 13 and 14 after meeting them in chat rooms. Costi was tracked down after the mother of another girl reported him to the Virtual Global Taskforce, a new international agency focused on online child abuse.

Yet there is very little hard information on just how many children are approached by adult predators when they are online or how many actually meet up with adults or take part in sexual activities in chat rooms or using webcams.

FIGURE 5.2 A news report claiming that "1 in 5 kids has been approached by online predators."

One statistic that is often quoted is that it is as high as one in five, and if this were true then it would be reason enough for anyone to keep their children from using the Internet (**FIGURE 5.3**).

The number actually comes from a report published in the United States in 2000, the University of New Hampshire's Crimes Against Children Research Center's online victimisation study. They interviewed

1,501 young people aged between 10 and 17 and, based on their results, they claimed that "approximately one in five received a sexual solicitation or approach over the Internet in the last year." They also pointed out that "one in thirty-three received an *aggressive* solicitation—a solicitor who asked to meet them somewhere; called them on the telephone; sent them regular mail, money or gifts".

The study also pointed out that:

- many—probably most—of those solicitations came from other teenagers
- "In 75 per cent of incidents, youth had no or only minor reactions, saying they were not very upset or afraid in the wake of the solicitation"
- "None of the solicitations led to an actual sexual contact or assault."

We know that children do meet up with friends that they have made on the Internet. A survey of primary school children in the UK by the Cyberspace Research Unit of the University of Lancashire found that 3 per cent of 8–11-year-olds had attended such a meeting, and more detailed research carried out for the UK Children Go Online project found that 8 per cent of 9–19-year-olds had done so.

These meetings were overwhelmingly positive in outcome and posed no danger. Nearly two thirds (65 per cent) of the meetings were with someone of about the same age, and a similar proportion (63 per cent) reported that the meeting had been suggested by both parties. Only 1 in 20 had not told anyone that they were going to a meeting, and three quarters (75 per cent) had told a parent. And 3 out of 5 (58 per cent) said that they had a good time.

When it comes to crimes against children, the only acceptable number is zero. But while we must always be vigilant about adults who prey on children, we shouldn't let that risk keep us from addressing more likely risks, including teenager-to-teenager sexual solicitations, which, in some cases, can also be extremely disturbing or extremely dangerous.

We spoke to one of the authors of the UNH study, Janis Wolak, and she said: "What puts kids at risk is when they talk about sex with the people they meet online. But the vast majority of kids won't get involved in that kind of situation."

All of which tells us that most teenagers, at least to some extent, say they're practising what we safety experts are preaching: not responding to these sexual messages and, as our children would put it, "ignoring the weirdos."

Actions Speak Louder. . .

Having said that, we need to look not just at what teenagers say about online safety but what they do. Isabelle (not her real name), a 15-year-old MySpace user who lives in Cambridge, is typical of many teenagers who pretend that they are more careful than they really are. When asked if she would add someone she doesn't know as a friend she said that she wouldn't, unless they were "a friend of a friend, maybe, if the friend had a good opinion of them", but then remembered that "I've got Solana's cousin as one of my friends—but he's a bit weird".

In April 2006 the US documentary show *Dateline* featured an investigation into how easy it is to persuade teenagers to trust people they don't know on MySpace.

Police officer, Frank Dannahay, set up a MySpace profile claiming to be a 19-year-old boy named Matt who had just moved into town. With very little effort he persuaded more than 100 people to add him to their MySpace friends list. Three of those "friends", teenage girls, appeared on the programme. Prior to meeting "Matt" on air, all three girls insisted that they took precautions before adding friends. One said "You don't put, like, your full name out there. You know, where you live. I don't add people I don't know. I don't, you know, talk to people I don't know," and the others agreed. Another girl told the interviewer, "If people, like, talk to me that I don't know, then I just, I don't talk to them."

When "Matt" walked into the room, the girls were shocked to discover that he was actually an adult policeman. Based on what he had learned about them online, Detective Dannahey was able to show the girls (and the TV audience) that he knew their full names, birthdays, where they lived and where they hung out after school. And these are girls who thought they were being careful.

Assessing the Risks

The most extreme risks, in terms of consequences, generally are the least likely, but that's no reason to abandon caution. Although the chances of your child's being forced into a physically abusive situation as a result of an online encounter are low, online socialisers face other dangers: the kind of stuff that has been going on in school canteens, classrooms, toilets, and playgrounds for generations. Now it happens online, too—everything from pranks and mean gossip to insults, threats and impersonation, to compromising party videos and overexposure, to self-published child porn.

Children are also being exposed to a constant barrage of sexually charged images from the profiles and websites of other teenagers on social networks, as well as in the adverts and programming of conventional media.

"The more often a person is exposed to these themes, the more normal it seems and the more desensitising it becomes," said Dr Sharon Cooper, forensic pediatrician and adjunct Professor of Pediatrics at the University of North Carolina. Dr Cooper also worries about some of the language that is becoming commonplace in popular culture. "Kids have started referring to themselves in sexually derogatory terms associated with prostitution."

Most of these dangers aren't life-threatening, but in some cases they can have an enormous impact on a child's self-esteem and, potentially, his or her future. Cyberbullying is the most common "risk" for junior-school-age social networkers. And privacy and protecting reputations is the biggest issue for secondary-school-age kids and university students.

Let's look at some of the more dangerous risks, beginning with the ones we fear most.

Adult Predators

Physical abuse, along with abduction, is a parent's worst nightmare. What we know about this terrible scenario is that abduction and rape resulting from an online encounter are highly unlikely.

Research carried out by the London School of Economics as part of the UK Children Go Online project found that one third of 9–19-year-olds daily and weekly net users have received unwanted sexual comments online or by text message, but few of these encounters lead to physical abuse. The most likely online scenario leading to a sexual encounter is that children will be lured into online conversation with someone they meet online and then be persuaded, perhaps over time, to meet that person offline and engage in sexual activity. This is illegal even if no abuse takes place–Section 15 of the Sexual Offences Act 2003 makes it an offence for an adult who has established contact with a child on at least two occasions to meet, or travel with the intention of meeting a child, with intent to commit a sexual offence against that child–but the sexual activity is rarely forced.

KEY PARENTING POINT

Teenagers may be naïve about the consequences of having sex with an adult but not necessarily blind to what they are doing. Only a small minority of offenders hide their intentions, as we mentioned earlier in the chapter. So for parents and law enforcement officials, a big part of the battle is not so much protecting children against attack as protecting them against their own misjudgement.

To prevent our children from becoming compliant victims, we need to teach them to be alert when in public online and to understand the risks of engaging in communications with people they don't know. That requires critical thinking and an understanding about how people try to manipulate children in seemingly benign ways.

Though this may seem more challenging than just teaching children to avoid physically dangerous situations, instilling mere awareness (of potential manipulation and danger) in them can go a long way towards ensuring safe, constructive social networking online and also in their offline encounters.

How Predators Groom Their Victims

Predators can be extremely skilled and patient, taking the time to groom their victims by paying them compliments or offering an understanding shoulder to lean on. In some cases, they also try intimidation.

Some of the things that predators say may look similar to what real friends might say, but if your children get comments or questions like these from someone they don't know, they should recognise them as signs to be a bit suspicious.

We've developed some "lines" that can help parents and children recognise predators. These lines are based on our own observations and on a report on cyberstalking and grooming published in June 2004 by the University of Central Lancashire. "Cyber Stalking, Abusive Cyber Sex, and Online Grooming" identifies common grooming techniques, and is based mostly on the kind of grooming that goes on in chat rooms.

- **"Where's your computer in the house?"** If the answer is "my bedroom," it tells the person that the parents are less likely to be in the room.

- **"What's your favourite band/designer/film/gear?"** Questions like these tell the groomer more about a child so that the groomer knows what gifts to offer: concert tickets, a webcam, software, clothes, CDs, and so on.

- **"I know someone who can get you a modelling job."** Flattery, groomers figure, will get them everywhere.

- **"I know a way you can earn money fast."** This line is one of the tactics that snagged 13-year-old Justin Berry into what became his webcam prostitution business, which Kurt Eichenwald wrote about in the *New York Times* on December 19, 2005 ("Through His webcam, a Boy Joins a Sordid Online World").

- **"You seem sad. Tell me what's bothering you."** This line is a sympathy ploy that can help turn a predator into a confidant.

▶

- **"What's your phone number?"** Asking for personal info of any kind usually happens at a later stage, after the target is feeling comfortable with the groomer. All kids who go online should know not to give out personal info online.

- **"If you don't [do what I ask], I'll [tell your parents *or* share your photos in a photo blog, webcam directory, or file-sharing network]."** Intimidation usually begins later, as the groomer learns more and more about the target.

- **"You are the love of my life."** This line is what "Amy," 15, fell for before travelling to meet someone who'd groomed her (quoted in "Amy's Story," a 2002 feature article in the Teens section of child safety site Netsmartz.org).

Surveys and Questionnaires

One way to teach awareness is to explain to children how predators groom their victims. One predator technique is to harvest as much information as possible about kids so that they can more easily manipulate them. Too much information makes the predator's job way too easy.

For example, surveys can provide an enormous amount of material at one glance. MySpace encourages users to complete an official profile questionnaire that asks about interests and favourite music, movies, and TV shows, as well as religion, habits, and sexual preference. Children do not have to fill out these questionnaires. Some kids actually (probably wisely) fictionalise their answers to throw off observers who aren't their friends.

There are also some very popular third-party surveys that children can fill out and post to their pages. Some of these surveys ask a lot of personal questions about likes, dislikes, personal feelings, drug and alcohol use, and sexual practices. The answers to such questions, if viewed by a would-be predator, could be used to exploit potential victims. In general, these surveys are not endorsed by MySpace but can be inserted into a profile using HTML code (see Chapter 7 for examples of these surveys and more information).

Special Risks for Some Children

One size never fits all. And while our general advice applies to the vast majority of young people, it doesn't apply to everyone. That's where parents come in. It's your job to assess your child's unique needs and proceed accordingly.

There are some teenagers who are particularly vulnerable and may need a bit of extra attention from parents when they're online. Adrien Survol Rivin, a clinical social worker who specialises in treating adolescents, worries about kids who are very compliant. "Children who are compliant in the real word," according to Rivin, "are more likely to act out by being non-compliant when they're online."

Part of being non-compliant is taking chances, such as entering into conversations with people they meet online. But, when under the influence of a predator, such children revert back to their old compliant selves because, says Rivin, "that's what they're used to, and they don't know how to be anything but compliant."

Paradoxically, she also worries about the "perfect kid." "If a kid is being perfect it may be that there are things that can't be expressed, so they have to go outside of the real word to find a place to break out of that mould. Often there is a certain level of excitement and danger that goes along with this." Predators know how to take advantage of such children, giving them the acceptance that they seek. Another issue with "perfect kids," said Rivin, is that "parents tend not to worry about them. They're excelling in school, music, sports and other activities, so it's easy for a parent to assume that everything is fine."

Still, says Dr Richard Toft, a child psychologist from California, "most kids are capable of knowing where to draw the line between online and offline relationships. There is a point were you have to move your body out of that chair and into the street, and that's a big step that most kids just won't take."

Harassment and Cyberbullying

Harassing peers in the process of figuring out where one stands in the social pecking order is nothing new. It's mostly a pre-teen and young teenager phenomenon. Cyberbullying is its online version, and it has become just as serious. It can include teasing kids about their appearance, sexuality, or other attributes; attempting to embarrass a child through the use of text, photos, video, and other media; and in some cases, threats and physical intimidation. There have been cases of children creating websites with the sole purpose of harassing schoolmates and even trying to taunt them into committing suicide. Bullying can take place via email, chat rooms, IM, websites, interactive online games, social-networking sites, and mobile phones. Sometimes, it spills over into the "real world."

Dealing with cyberbullying can be tough. In some cases, teachers or police can help, but if no laws are being broken, the police can't step in.

One thing is for sure: your kids need to understand that if they're mistreated by others, it's not their fault.

Advice for Dealing with Cyberbullies

The Canadian website Cyberbullying.org recommends the following tips for children when dealing with bullying online.

- **Don't reply to messages from cyberbullies.** Even though you may want to respond, this is exactly what cyberbullies want. They want to know that they've got you worried and upset. They are trying to mess with your mind and control you—to put fear into you. Don't give them that pleasure.

- **Do not keep this to yourself!** You are *not* alone, and you did *not* do anything to deserve the bullying. Tell an adult you know and trust about the situation.

- **Inform your Internet service provider (ISP) or mobile phone provider.**

- **Inform your local police.** Do this with a parent's help, if the behaviour seems to call for it.

- **Do not erase or delete messages from cyberbullies.** You don't have to read the messages, but keep them; they are your evidence. Unfortunately, you may get similar messages again, perhaps from other accounts. If they're involved, the police, your ISP, and/or your mobile phone provider can use these messages to help you.

Don't Let Your Own Children Be Cyberbullies

Most cases of cyberbullying involve children as perpetrators as well as victims, so it's important to make sure that your children aren't bullying others.

In "A Parents' Guide to Cyberbullying and Cyberthreats" (Center for Safe & Responsible Internet Use, December 2005), author Nancy Willard recommends that parents discuss with their young people "the value of treating others with kindness and respect and about your expectation that your child will act in accord with these values online." She also recommends that parents institute repercussions and enforce them when their child "engages in irresponsible online behaviour."

Privacy and Security

We discussed in Chapter 2 the issue of teenagers labouring under what may be a false sense of privacy and security. To them it may seem like this is just "kid space" but it's not. Even young people who say they never give out personal information in chat rooms have told us they feel more comfortable revealing that information on MySpace, even though what they post can be seen, used, or shared by virtually anyone (unless they have a private profile).

Though we suspect that this situation is changing because of the enormous publicity about social-networking risks, we have spoken with numerous teenagers who still feel that MySpace truly is their space. MySpacers who told us that they would never post personal information in a chat room have argued that that rule shouldn't apply to social-networking sites, as though these sites somehow had a greater level of security than chat rooms.

But that's simply not true. Unless your children have a private profile (which is now an option for all users and the default for 14- and 15-year-olds), much of what they post on MySpace can be seen by virtually anyone. So even if their intentions are to communicate with their friends, they need to be aware that they have more "friends" than they realised.

What teenagers post in online public spaces without regard for their privacy and future prospects is the social Web's most common risk for secondary school and university-age people. Parents are right to be concerned about this because, at the time of writing, there isn't much evidence that teenage social networkers are thinking about it enough: young people need to think before they post. They need to consider whether or not they want a prospective employer, for example, to see what they're posting about themselves and their friends. Google, Yahoo!, and MSN Search aren't the only places where people can search for them. Social-network search boxes aren't just used to find friends, but also potential university students, employees, or anyone doing "background checks." There's also a permanent Internet Archive (more about that in a minute).

What young people need to think about (and parents can help them think about) is the "you-can't-take-it-back" issue. Once something's on a website or sent to a friend via a mobile phone, IM, or email, it's out of their control.

A friend can copy 'n' paste, pass it along, or upload it to a myriad of sites and services. It may be something a friend shares unthinkingly, or it might be passed along as a joke or maliciously, by an ex-friend who somehow got the originator's IM or email password.

KEY PARENTING POINT

For younger MySpacers, it would be ideal for parents to be on their childrens' friends lists, the better to monitor what's going on in their online social lives. But at least consider a family rule that friends lists are only for people whom both the children and a parent know in real life.

Privacy is a Double-edged Sword

In June 2006 MySpace changed its privacy policy to allow anyone, including users 16 or older, to create a private profile.

Though we agree that people should have the right to privacy features, it's also important to point out that privacy is a double-edged sword. The upside is that privacy features can make your child's profile visible only to people on his or her friends list.

▶

The downside is that parents may want to see their childrens' profiles too. They need to be aware that privacy features can also block them unless they're on their childrens' friends lists. There have been some calls to require social-networking sites to notify parents when minors set up a social-networking profile, but, at the time of writing, we are not aware of any specific legislation, nor are we sure how it would work.

A public profile makes it harder for teenagers to carry on underground conversations, which can support or reinforce destructive behaviours such as anorexia, self-mutilation, discrimination, violence, or alcohol or drug abuse in children who are troubled and seeking that kind of "support."

You may have heard about one well-publicised case in the US, in which five teenage boys used their public MySpace accounts to trumpet their intention to shoot up their school. An adult woman spotted the page and alerted authorities, who found the boys' weapons. A few media reports actually "blamed" MySpace, but the public MySpace profile and the alert woman might actually have helped prevent a tragedy. Of course, MySpace and other social networks aren't the only places where troubled teenagers can get reinforcement from others with similar inclinations.

The Permanent Internet Archive

Even when no one goes out of the way to hold on to what you post, it can still hang around forever. Google, for example, has a temporary "cache" of web pages that have been changed or deleted. There's also a site called the "Internet Archive" (archive.org) that is archiving almost everything on the Web to "offer permanent access for researchers, historians, and scholars," the site says. It doesn't matter to them that your child's MySpace profile isn't a *Times* editorial. It's part of the Internet and, thanks to this non-profit service, it's potentially enshrined forever (**FIGURE 5.3**).

FIGURE 5.3 The Internet Archive's "WayBackMachine" can resurrect 55 billion defunct web pages.

People can ask the archive to remove their pages, providing they have those pages' URLs. If children find their pages (by typing the URL into the archive's search box on its home page), they can email the archive (see its FAQ) with the URL, requesting deletion. Allow for "about a two-day turn-around," the Internet Archive's spokesperson told us.

Phishing and Malicious Software

Many children have access to credit or debit cards that should be shared only with legitimate merchants. Children as well as adults can fall victim to *"phishing"* schemes, in which they get an email that appears to come from a legitimate organisation but that contains links to a rogue website (one that is not what it appears to be or says it is). Information that you provide to a rogue site can be used to steal your identity, break into your online accounts, and/or withdraw money from your various accounts (**FIGURE 5.5**).

There is even the risk of phishing within social networking. One visitor to our BlogSafety.com forum reported that his son visited a profile containing a link to a picture or video. When the boy clicked the link, what looked like a MySpace page popped up, saying, "You need to be logged in to do that." So he logged back in (or thought he did). But instead of giving his password to MySpace, he unknowingly gave it to a

FIGURE 5.5 This looks just like PayPal's home page, but the URL at the top doesn't say paypal.com. Any information you type could well go to a criminal who can use it to break into your account.

fake site that looked just like MySpace, meaning that his personal info fell into the hands of criminals. Someone used the young man's account name and password to impersonate him and create a malicious profile about him on another website.

KEY PARENTING POINT

Whether a phishing attack comes via email, IM, MySpace, or any other means, the safest way to log into a website where you're asked for a password, credit card numbers, or any other confidential information is to type the Web address (URL) of the site yourself, rather than clicking on a link to it.

The Art of Creating a Password

Many people worry about hackers stealing passwords, but in reality, many people in effect give them away by being careless.

Common mistakes are choosing passwords that are easy to guess, using the same passwords for all the sites you visit, and sometimes allowing other people to know your passwords. We know of a case in which a 13-year-old girl emailed sexually explicit photos of herself to a boy who had shared his email password with a "friend." That friend proceeded to find the photos and post them on a public web page he created just to hurt the girl's reputation.

One simple way to pick a hard-to-guess password is to make up a phrase you can remember but others would never guess, and then base your password on letters and numbers from that phrase—for example, a phrase like "I started at Kingswood School in '03" to generate the tough-to-guess password IsaKSi03. It's also a good idea to not use the same password on all sites and definitely not to use important passwords (such as the MySpace one) on sites you don't fully trust.

KEY PARENTING POINT

Tell your children why it's important not to let their friends have their passwords. Friends don't always stay friends—and they can be careless with passwords and share them with people your children may not even know. Friends can also play pranks (like sharing very personal info from or impersonating someone who shared their password) and get people in trouble, mistakenly or to be mean—such as the case of the 13-year-old girl we just mentioned.

Updates and Security Software

We won't go into a lot of detail here, but everyone who uses the Internet should protect their PC by making sure it has the latest updates and by using security software that helps prevent a variety of problems, including viruses, spyware, and worms that install code that takes control of your PC or steals your passwords and credit card info. Windows security programs are available from a variety of companies, including McAfee, Microsoft, Trend Micro, and Zone Alarm. Symantec offers security software for both Windows and Macintosh (**FIGURE 5.6**).

You'll find more security tips at www.blogsafety.net/parentbook.

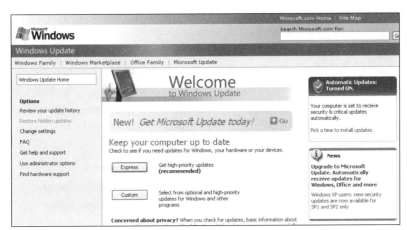

FIGURE 5.6 Microsoft's Windows Update page at update.microsoft.com automatically scans Windows PCs to make sure they have the latest security updates.

Legal Risks and School Policies

Children aren't just victims of crime and harassment; they can be perpetrators as well. They need to be reminded that there are consequences to their online behaviour. In addition to being wrong and rude, using the Internet to harass or annoy others can get your children into trouble with school authorities or even the law. Young people should also know that there is a line between online "flirting" and sexual harassment that should not be crossed. Most parents have a pretty good idea where that line is, so as uncomfortable as it may be, it's a good idea to talk with your children about it.

The same is true of other online infringements, such as hacking, invading others' privacy, planting viruses, or posting libellous or slanderous information, as well as copyright infringements. Young people also need to be aware that what they post on the Net can be used against them, now or in the future. There are numerous cases of police and schools taking action against young people based on information posted on MySpace and other social networks or revealed in chat rooms or via email.

Parents and children should check the Internet-use policies that apply in their schools. Schools have filters in place to stop children accessing unsuitable material when they are in class or working in the library, and these may block access to MySpace or other social-networking sites but, even if your children can reach these sites, they should be careful not to break school policy on viewing or posting unsuitable material. If a ban is in place, and we don't necessarily agree that banning MySpace is a good idea, then your children should know about it as they could be in trouble if they break the rules.

In the US there have been cases of colleges and even schools monitoring MySpace and Facebook profiles for evidence of underage drinking or illegal drug use, although this does not seem to be something schools in the UK do.

However the police may be about to take an interest, since the *Belfast Telegraph* reported in August 2006 that the recently revived rave scene, with illegal parties being held in fields or disused properties, is being coordinated on MySpace, with DJs and organisers using the site to tell people where and when to meet.

Exposure to Inappropriate Material

Posting or viewing text, photos, and videos that are inappropriate for children is less an issue on MySpace and most legitimate social-networking sites than it is on the Web in general.

First, MySpace policy prohibits "photographs containing nudity, or obscene, lewd, excessively violent, harassing, sexually explicit or otherwise objectionable subject matter." Of course it's possible for such material to sneak past the company's censors, but if it's found, it's removed.

Second, we're not saying there isn't material in MySpace that some parents would find objectionable for their teenagers, but there are plenty of other places on the Net where they are more likely to find this material.

A lot has been said and written about exposure to material such as pornography that can be considered "harmful to minors". Britain has an Obscene Publications Act that applies online as well as offline, and the Protection of Children Act 1978 makes it a criminal offence to "take, permit to be taken, make, possess, show, distribute or advertise indecent images of children" in the United Kingdom. In addition there have recently been proposals to make it a criminal offence to possess pornography that involves extreme violence.

Online pornography is a multibillion-dollar business, and although many porn sites require credit card access for much of their material, there is plenty out there that kids can find for free, including photos, stories, and videos. There are even pornographic videos that can be downloaded to iPods and game players.

Child Pornography

Although any form of pornography can be disturbing, especially if seen by young children, there is a legal (and, we would argue, moral) distinction between adult pornography and images of child abuse, sometimes called "child pornography". Much sexually explicit material on the Internet is legal but an exception is made for indecent photographs of children. As we have pointed out, the Protection of Children Act 1978 makes the creation, distribution or possession of such images a criminal offence.

As so often in English law, the exact definition of the words involved is left vague. According to the Internet Watch Foundation, the word 'indecent' should be taken at its dictionary meaning; as a guide it means "any images of children, apparently under 18 years of age, involved in sexual activity or posed to be sexually provocative."

The Internet Watch Foundation website is at www.iwf.org.uk and they run a hotline where people can report such images if they come across them online.

KEY PARENTING POINT

We've noticed a small but growing number of "self-published child porn" cases. That's our term for when children take sexually explicit and/or nude photos of themselves and email, IM, or upload them to websites, often with no concept of the potential impact on their lives if this material is passed around. Laws haven't caught up with this new phenomenon, and prosecutors around the country are wrestling with the issue. But according to Mary Leary, deputy director of the

National Center for Missing & Exploited Children's Office of Legal Counsel,
"Kids face the possibility of charges much more so now than in the past."

If Your Kids Are Viewing Pornography . . .

Adult pornography, although legal, can be disturbing. But how you
respond to a child's exposure to it should depend on several factors,
including the age and maturity of your child, how he or she encounters it,
how much time is spent looking at it and how it is affecting your child.

Overreacting generally is the worst response, because it tends to
make them take cover and become less communicative at a time when
communication is really needed.

What's a Parent to Do?

In addressing a worried nation on the eve of his first term in office in 1933,
US President Franklin D. Roosevelt famously said, "The only thing we
have to fear is fear itself—nameless, unreasoning, unjustified terror which
paralyses needed efforts to convert retreat into advance."

His advice couldn't be more relevant. Fear does paralyse. Parental
fears shut down communication and make teenagers want to be as far
away from their parents as they can possibly get. It has never been more
important for that *not* to happen.

Trust between parent and child is needed more now simply because
of the enormous number of options they have online, with no mitigating
factor or fallback *but* their parents. The bottom line: because there are
so many "places" they can go online that we don't know about, the best
way to know about where they're going—the one that fosters trust and
cooperation—is if they tell us about them.

This chapter has hopefully provided you a hype-free consideration of
the research on online child exploitation; a clear-eyed view of all the risks
associated with young people's use of the Web past and present; and
what's newly risky on Web 2.0.

In the next chapter, we'll give you the "toolkit"—some tips, tools, and
our best sense of how to parent young explorers of the social Web.

CHAPTER 6

A Parents' Toolkit

At the risk of seeming overly simplistic, the best way to protect your children on MySpace or anywhere else is to talk with them—not only about risks, but also about the positive things they do online, what they do and don't like about social networking, and how you feel about it. Keep in mind they don't need us (or our credit cards) to use MySpace, but, as is usually the case in teenage lives, they need us as a sounding board.

It's important that your communication with your child is two-way—listen to them, be supportive, and keep an open mind. Whatever you do, don't overreact, and try to keep a sense of proportion. In most cases, the first response to a problem shouldn't be to punish children or even ban their use of MySpace or the Internet, but to discuss the issue to see if there are solutions you can agree on.

Keeping children safe online isn't about technology; it's about parenting. You know how to do that, regardless of how tech savvy you are (or aren't).

Children Want Parental Input

Some people think that children don't value their parents' opinions, but data suggests that this isn't true. In 2005 a panel of 4,000 readers of *The Times* and *The Sunday Times* was asked about the factors influencing their childrens' choice of career, and parents were seen as by far the most important (74 per cent), followed by teachers (62 per cent). In the United States a March 2006 survey of 46,000 13–18-year-olds carried out by Boys *&* Girls Clubs of America found that nearly half (48 per cent) of teenagers felt their parents and guardians "significantly influence their decisions".

Keeping an open line of communication shouldn't happen just during special times when you and your children sit down to talk about Internet safety; it's about your entire relationship. How you talk with your children about everything, your interest in their activities, and conversations over dinner are all part of how we parents help our children grow into adults. At the end of the day, Internet safety isn't about rules; it's about critical thinking skills. Children need to learn to think for themselves—to protect themselves and to internalise those values that will help transform them into safe, careful, and caring adults.

In addition to communicating openly with your children, we recommend sharing some online guidelines. "Safe Blogging Tips for Teens" (from BlogSafety.com) lists six guidelines (see right). If you want to keep things really simple, make sure your kids are aware of the two cardinal rules of online safety:

- never reveal personally identifiable information, such as your name, address, or phone number (including your mobile phone number)
- be extremely careful about face-to-face meetings with people you meet online.

BlogSafety.com also offers social-networking tips for parents (see page 134).

Safe Blogging Tips for Teens

(from BlogSafety.com)

Be as anonymous as possible. Avoid posting information that could enable a stranger to locate you. That information includes your last name, the name of your school, teams you play for, the town you live in, and where you hang out.

Protect your information. Check to see if your service has a friends list that allows you to control who can visit your profile or blog. If so, allow only people you know and trust. If you don't use privacy features, anyone can see your information, including people with bad intentions.

Avoid in-person meetings. Don't get together with someone you "meet" in a profile or blog unless you are certain of his or her actual identity. Although it's still not risk free, if you do meet the person, arrange the meeting in a public place, and bring some friends along.

Photos: think before posting. What's uploaded to the Net can be downloaded by anyone and passed around or posted online pretty much forever. Avoid posting photos that allow people to identify you (for example, when they're searching for your school), especially sexually suggestive images. Before uploading a photo, think about how you'd feel if it were seen by a parent or grandparent, university admissions tutor, or future employer.

Check comments regularly. If you allow comments on your profile or blog, check them often. Don't respond to mean or embarrassing comments. Delete them, and if possible, block offensive people from commenting further.

Be honest about your age. Membership rules exist to protect people. If you are too young to sign up, do not attempt to lie about your age. Talk with your parents about alternative sites that may be appropriate for you.

Social-networking Tips for Parents

(from BlogSafety.com)

In addition to laying down some guidelines for children, we also have some tips for parents.

- **Be reasonable, and try to set reasonable expectations.**
  Pulling the plug on children's Internet activities is rarely a good first response to a problem; it's too easy for them to go underground and establish free messaging and social-networking accounts at a friend's house or many other places.

- **Be open with your teenage children,** and encourage them to come to you if they encounter a problem online. Cultivate trust and communication; no rules, laws, or filtering software can replace you as their first line of defence. Teaching your children to be critical thinkers about their safety will pay dividends for years to come.

- **Talk with your children** about how they use the services. Make sure that they understand basic Internet and social-networking safety guidelines. These include protecting privacy (including passwords), never posting personally identifying information, avoiding in-person meetings with people they meet online, and not posting inappropriate or potentially embarrassing photos. Suggest that they use the services' privacy tools to share information only with people they know from the real world and that they never admit "friends" to their pages unless they are certain who those people are.

- **Consider requiring that all online activity take place in a central area of the home,** not in a child's bedroom. Be aware that there are also ways children can access the Internet away from home, including on many phones, game players, and other portable devices.

- **Try to get your children to share their blogs or online profiles with you,** but be aware that they can have multiple accounts on multiple services. Use search engines and the search tools on social-networking sites to search for your child's full name, phone number, and other identifying information.

Privacy Options for Older Children

As we explained earlier, MySpace allows all users to create a private profile that can been viewed by only their friends. Users who are 16 years or older by default have public profiles, so if you have older children, there's a good chance that their profiles are public. We suggest that parents talk with their children about the pluses and minuses of having a private profile (see "Privacy Is a Double-edged Sword" in Chapter 5).

Reporting Misconduct on MySpace

If you're on someone's profile and see something that you consider to be inappropriate, you can report it to MySpace right from that page by clicking the Report Inappropriate Content link at the bottom of that page (**FIGURE 6.1**). The link takes you to a page where you can send an email to customer service.

About | FAQ | Terms | Privacy | Safety Tips | Contact MySpace | Report Inappropriate Content | Promote! | Advertise | MySpace International

FIGURE 6.1 To send a report to MySpace, click the Report Inappropriate Content link at the bottom of the person's profile. Click the Terms link to see what the site defines as inappropriate.

KEY PARENTING POINT

Inappropriate content comprises anything that violates MySpace's terms of use, which are spelled out on the site's Terms page. (To access that page, click the Terms link located at the bottom of most pages—see Figure 6.1). This type of content includes nudity or postings that are "excessively violent, harassing, sexually explicit or otherwise objectionable."

In addition to inappropriate content on people's profiles, there are other forms of misconduct that you should consider reporting, such as spam, underage users, cyberbullying, copyright violation, or anything else that you feel violates MySpace terms.

You can report misconduct by using the Contact MySpace link at the bottom of every page.

Follow these steps.

1. Click the Contact MySpace link (**FIGURE 6.2**).

FIGURE 6.2 Click Contact MySpace if you have a comment, question, or report to send the service.

The page that displays has two boxes at the top, one linking to the site's latest updates, and the other to the MySpace FAQ (**FIGURE 6.3**). MySpace really hopes you'll try to find what you're looking for before you send them email. You can look at the FAQ, but if you're writing about an abuse issue, it's not going to solve your problem.

Home | Browse | Search | Invite | Film | Mail | Blog | Favorites | Forum | Groups | Events | Videos | Music | Classifieds

Know what's going on without having to ask! Click here to read updates.

Your question probably already has an answer! Click here to read FAQ.

TOP 6 QUESTIONS

1. Is MySpace free?

2. How do I add color, graphics, & sound to my profile page?

3. How can I change my name, age, and/or add to the information on my profile?

4. How can I change my email address and/or password?

5. Why is my profile page suddenly messed up?

6. How do I report Identity theft, Underage User, Cyberbullying, or Copyright Violation to MySpace?

Contact Request

Questions, Comments, Concerns? We'd like to hear from you:

Subject: Please select a topic

Please select topic above

Submit

NOTE: Please choose "Cancel" from the Account Settings to delete your account. If you do not receive the confirmation e-mail for account deletion, please **email us** from the e-mail address you use on myspace.

We will not honor delete requests sent via this form.

FIGURE 6.3 You can send a report to MySpace using the Contact Request box.

2. Click the arrow beside the Subject field. When the list of topics displays, you'll probably want to select Reporting Abuse (**FIGURE 6.4**). Then click the Please Select a Subtopic message that pops up and click Submit.

A Preliminary Response to Question screen displays links to answers to commonly asked questions.

Contact Request

Questions, Comments, Concerns? We'd like to hear from you:

Subject: | Reporting Abuse ▼ |

| Cyberbullying ▼ |

[Submit]

NOTE: Please choose "Cancel" from the Account Settings to delete your account. If you do not receive the confirmation e-mail for account deletion, please **email us** from the e-mail address you use on myspace.

We will not honor delete requests sent via this form.

FIGURE 6.4 The pulldown menus require you to select a topic, and then a subtopic.

3. Assuming you still want to send the message, click No, Email Customer Service (**FIGURE 6.5**).

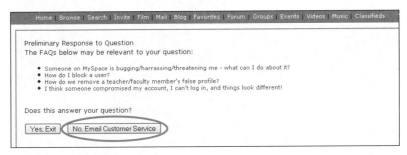

FIGURE 6.5 At last you can actually send your message.

4. Finally, you get to a page where you can type your note. If you're logged into MySpace, your name and email address are probably already there. If not, type them in, type your message in the Message box and click Submit Question (**FIGURE 6.6**).

KEY PARENTING POINT

If you are reporting what you believe to be a crime, or if there is any risk to life, property, or safety, contact the police as well. If it's a case of sexual exploitation of a child or suspected child pornography, go to the CEOP website at www.ceop.gov.uk or the Internet Watch Foundation at www.iwf.org.uk

FIGURE 6.6 Type your message to MySpace Customer Care staff.

Use Our BlogSafety Forum

We maintain an interactive forum at BlogSafety.com where you can ask questions and interact with others. Although the forum is not a hotline or a watchdog organisation, in many cases, you can get answers very quickly from us, other experts, or other parents—who are often the best experts around! If you report a serious problem on the forum, we will do our best to bring it to the attention of MySpace officials or advise you as to what we think you should do (**FIGURE 6.7**).

Finding Your Child Online

The ideal way to monitor your child's site is to visit it often and look around. If your child has a private profile, have him or her add you as a friend so you can check in every now and then. Ask for the URL (Web address) of their page. If your child doesn't give you that information, you may still be able to find it.

Searching for Your Child's Profile

If your child has a public profile, you—or anyone—can find his or her MySpace site, provided you know what to look for.

To access the MySpace search feature, follow these steps.

1. On any page in the site, click Search on the blue navigation bar at the top of the page. On the MySpace.com home page, you can also use the Search box on the right. If you use the Search box, first select the MySpace radio button under the text box, so you'll be searching only MySpace and not the entire Web (**FIGURE 6.8**).

FIGURE 6.8 Make sure you're just searching MySpace (if you're looking for a profile on it) by selecting the MySpace option, and then type your child's info into the Search field.

2. Type your child's name, email address, or what you think might be the display name or screen name (a kind of nickname) in the Search field, and then select either The Web or MySpace radio buttons beneath the Search field to indicate the parameters of your search (**FIGURE 6.9**).

TIP

In some cases, you may need to be a MySpace member to access information. If so, go ahead and sign up for a free account; you don't have to put any info in it.

| Home | Browse | Search | Invite | Film | Mail | Blog | Favorites | Forum | Groups | Eve |

MySpace Search

Search MySpace Profiles

Search [MySpace ▾] for [   ] [Search]

Find Someone You Know

⊞ Find a Friend

Select search by: ◉ Name ○ Display Name ○ Email

[Roberto Gonzales   ] [Find]

Example: Tom Jones *or* Tom *or* tjones@hotmail.com

FIGURE 6.9 MySpace search works like most Web search engines.

If the information you're searching for appears in your child's profile, you'll see a page where you can view the profile, if it's public, by clicking View Profile. If the profile is private, you will see some information but not the full profile (**FIGURE 6.10**).

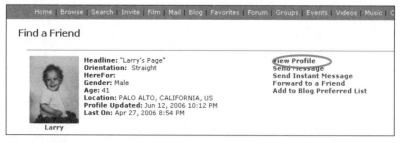

| Home | Browse | Search | Invite | Film | Mail | Blog | Favorites | Forum | Groups | Events | Videos | Music | C |

Find a Friend

Headline: "Larry's Page"
Orientation: Straight
HereFor:
Gender: Male
Age: 41
Location: PALO ALTO, CALIFORNIA, US
Profile Updated: Jun 12, 2006 10:12 PM
Last On: Apr 27, 2006 8:54 PM

Larry

(View Profile)
Send Message
Send Instant Message
Forward to a Friend
Add to Blog Preferred List

FIGURE 6.10 If your child's profile displays and is public, you can click on the blue "View Profile" link on the right to see what the rest of the world can see.

It is quite possible for your child to sign up under a different name, of course, or from an email address you may not be aware of (**FIGURE 6.11**). Some teenagers might decide to tell only certain friends their fictitious name or URL and "stealth" email address or IM screen name, and it'd

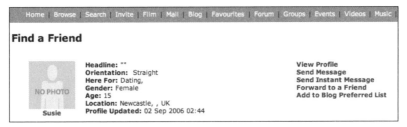

FIGURE 6.11 This fictitious 14-year-old, "Susie," has a private profile, but anyone can see her first name, gender, age, sexual orientation, location, and the fact she's "here for" dating. If she had posted a photo, it too would be displayed.

be tough for anyone else to find the profile. Anyone can get free email addresses and IM accounts from services like Hotmail, AIM, and Yahoo!.

You can also try searching MySpace, Google, and other search engines for other information, such as your child's mobile number, address, screen name, friends' names, school name, sports team names, or anything else that might show up on the Web or in a profile.

Browsing by School

Another way a parent might search for a son or daughter is to use the Classmate Finder option in MySpace's search area (**FIGURE 6.12**).

To use this option, do the following.

1. Type the school name in the Classmate Finder search box and also indicate the school's country.

2. When you find the school among your search results, you can narrow your search for your child by gender, age range, and whether your child is a current student or a graduate. You can also enter optional keywords (the names of clubs or teams he or she is a member of) on the right side (**FIGURE 6.13**).

Because some children lie about their ages, it's best to choose an age range—for example, from 16 to 100 (a lot of teenagers are pretty random about their "ages"—many just say "100").

FIGURE 6.12 Type your child's school name and other info into Classmate Finder.

FIGURE 6.13 Provide the search tool with as much info as you can think of to refine your search.

Alternatives for 'Tweens

MySpace personnel and site-monitoring technology do look for profiles of kids who appear to be younger than 14, and if they find or receive reports about those profiles, the profiles are deleted. But MySpace staff can't find all of those profiles, and a user whose profile is deleted can just create a new one. If you discover that your child under 14 has a MySpace profile, you can request that it be cancelled. But along with doing that, consider helping your child find another outlet for socialising that's more age-appropriate. For example, Imbee.com is a new social-networking site for kids 8 to 14 that includes parental controls, and AOL has a number of kids-only and teenager-only services and forums for its members (**FIGURE 6.14**).

Monitoring and Filtering

Because of concerns about MySpace, more and more parental-controls software companies are adding social-networking monitoring to either their products or their marketing of these products, and new MySpace-specific products are coming on the market. The line-up is changing fast, so for a comprehensive view of what's available, you'll need to do a product search in a Web search engine to get product ads or a list of search results. Search using phrases like "monitor MySpace," "blog monitoring," or "MySpace parental controls."

Monitoring Services

The most useful thing about the MySpace-specific services is that they alert you to changes to your child's profile, assuming that the profile is public.

KEY PARENTING POINT

There is an important difference between services that monitor changes to your child's public profile and monitoring software that records everything your kids do on the PC. The former is simply a convenient way for you to see what anyone else can see—what your kid is posting in public. PC monitoring software can be used to spy on everything your child types and sees, including private messages.

US-based MySpaceWatch.com, which is not affiliated with MySpace, offers both a free and a fee-based service to help you track what's happening in your childrens' profiles. The free version will monitor one profile and crawl (look for updates) twice a day. The $6-per-month version monitors up to five profiles and provides a list of your child's friends and updates every six hours (**FIGURE 6.15**).

Services like this provide limited information, but they do make it easy to get updates, assuming that your child is registered under his or her real name or an email address you know about. There is also the possibility that you're spending a lot of time monitoring only *one* of your child's accounts, and it may even be the one he or she intended you to see. That children can establish multiple accounts on multiple services is a distinct limitation of these products. They can give you a false sense of security.

MySpaceWatch and other monitoring sites may seem to offer a quick way of finding out what your teenagers are up to online, but knowing how MySpace works yourself is a much better approach. If you do sign up for one of these services, check it out carefully beforehand, as you will be giving them access to a lot of personal information about your child.

FIGURE 6.15 The paid version of myspaceWatch lets you view a summary of your child's profile, get updates on comments, and see who your child's "friends" are.

Monitoring Software

Monitoring software can log and report to you everything your child is doing on that particular computer—all the keystrokes, whether in IM or email, on social networks or other websites, or in word-processing and other programs.

One problem with monitoring software is that, like filters, they can't be everywhere; they work only on the machine where they're installed. As the Internet becomes available in more and more places and on growing numbers of portable devices, "parental control" software is getting less helpful.

An even greater potential problem is that monitoring can lead to distrust if your child knows or suspects you are "spying" on everything happening on the PC. We're not here to judge the choice you make. All parents need to do what's appropriate for their families, but we urge you to be very thoughtful before installing monitoring software or signing on with a monitoring service. If you do decide to use it, consider telling your children you've installed it so that they know it's there; they might figure it out anyway.

"Tracking software presupposes a lack of trust between parent and child, and it is very difficult to go back. Indeed, this is a 'last resort' approach," wrote parent and technology educator Jeff Cooper in our BlogSafety.com forum. We agree.

If you're interested in using monitoring software, the leading provider is SpectorSoft. Another is (appropriately named?) IamBigBrother (**FIGURE 6.16**).

FIGURE 6.16 For better or worse, IamBigBrother lets you "see everything your family is doing online."

Filtering

Numerous programs are available that are designed to *filter* the Web (block users from visiting certain types of sites on your home computer).

Software like CYBERsitter, Net Nanny, CyberPatrol, and Norton Parental Controls generally do a good job of keeping children away from porn, hateful messages, and other areas of the Web that parents want to keep off limits. You can also configure most of these programs to add or remove sites, so it's possible to use one of these programs to keep your children from visiting MySpace (and many are adding social networking to their lists of blocked sites).

As you might have guessed, we don't recommend that you filter out social-networking sites, especially for teenagers, for several reasons.

- All you would accomplish would be to block your children on the computer at home. Filters will do nothing to keep them from visiting the sites on other computers or on mobile phones or other devices.

- Although these filters can be effective in keeping small children from visiting certain types of sites accidentally, they are pretty useless when it comes to computer-savvy teenagers who can probably find a way around them. Plenty of proxy sites help in-the-know children bypass any filters that their parents or schools put on a computer or network. Sites like UnblockMe and HideUS (and there are many more) allow users to go anywhere they want, despite filters and without detection.

- As we've mentioned several times throughout this book, even if you could keep your children from using MySpace, you might wind up driving them to other, less accountable or more dangerous sites, in effect encouraging them to go underground for their social networking.

Cancelling Your Child's Account

If you feel you must cancel your child's MySpace account, that is certainly your right as a parent. However, the only easy way to do that is with your child's cooperation.

In its Frequently Asked Questions, MySpace suggests, "Please work with your child to remove the account." That advice may seem to be unhelpful, but cooperation is important. Even if your child does agree to remove his or her profile, there is nothing to stop them from setting up a new profile that might be even harder for you to find—or setting up an account on another social-networking service.

The Email Issue

Sometimes, children set up accounts by using a fake email address. If the child is cooperative, and you've followed the basic account-cancellation steps but haven't received the confirmation email that's supposed to come within 24 hours, log into the child's profile and delete all the information in it (Headline, About Me, Interests, and so on). Then type in one of those boxes, "Remove this profile."

Next, send an email to CustomerCare@MySpace.com. In that email, provide the URL (Web address) of your child's account, such as www. myspace.com/susiemsith or www.myspace.com/99999999. (The URL is displayed in the My URL box of the user's home page, just below the Hello box.)

Next in your email, state that you want the profile to be removed and that the profile is now blank except for the instruction to remove it.

Without Your Child's Help

If you can't get into the account, send an email to "deleteaccount@ myspace.com" with the profile's URL and ask that the profile be deleted. Without that URL, MySpace has no way of knowing which of the millions of profiles belongs to your child. If you don't know the address, try searching for it in MySpace's search box, using information such as your child's first and last names, school name, friends' URLs or names, as we describe in "Finding Your Child Online," earlier in this chapter. If there's evidence in the profile that the child is younger than MySpace's minimum age of 14, MySpace will delete the account—usually, within 48 hours of verification. In any case, you will receive an automated email providing a number that you can call to discuss your case.

Impersonators

If you can't get into the account because someone else created it to impersonate, embarrass, or otherwise harass your child, MySpace says, "We remove it on sight." Just email customercare@myspace.com to request deletion, again with the URL or address of the profile.

But keep in mind that realistically, there aren't enough hours in a day, week, or month in parents' schedules to find and, if desired, take down every account their children have established online. It's better to work with your children on safe online socialising than to ban it and, in the process, send them into stealth mode. Open MySpace use, with ground rules, is much safer!

Your Best Defence. . .

While you may be heartened to learn of all the tools available to help keep kids safe on MySpace, remember what we said at the start of the chapter: your best tool is maintaining an open relationship with your children.

And here's another piece of advice you probably didn't expect to find in a book about MySpace: one way to help your children stay safe online is to have meals together as a family. We all lead busy lives, and it's very easy to just grab food on our own. But family mealtimes are a chance to talk, process your day, and just be together. We're not suggesting that you talk about MySpace at dinner (lest you choke on your food), just that you spend time together and take interest in each other's lives. It's what relationships—and parenting—are all about.

CHAPTER 7

MySpacers' Advanced Tricks and Tips

TRICKS FOR CUSTOMISING MYSPACE may seem a bit much to many parents, but millions of children are customising and doing a whole lot more to their spaces. That they should want to use tools to spiff up their pages should come as no surprise. MySpace profiles aren't just websites, as we mentioned in Chapter 2. They're one avenue children use to express themselves, show off, make friends, one-up their friends, and create and recreate their online identities.

We don't expect many parents will want to implement the tricks featured in this chapter. But by reading through it you'll get a good idea of what a lot of children are doing. Maybe you'll even discover a trick or two you can pass on to your family and score a point or two!

Pimping and Hacking: Oh My!

A common phrase related to customising that MySpace users like to throw around is "Pimp Your MySpace." We're not exactly thrilled by the choice of words, since "pimp" is a term associated with the exploitation of women. Even so, and thanks largely to the popular MTV show *Pimp My Ride*, the term has taken on a new connotation that means something like "customise," but it's really more than that. It's the process of personalising one's space so that it's not just unique but pretty flashy.

Another word you might have heard teenagers use a lot is "hacks." Though the term "hacker" is commonly used to describe criminals who break into computer systems, it's also a term of endearment used to describe savvy computer users who figure out clever ways to make products and websites do incredible things. There are plenty of "MySpace hacks" that allow users to customise their pages. So as offensive as "pimp" is to some and "hacks" to others, in the world of MySpace they are seen by many as good things than can bring extra status to those who master them.

HTML Is Key

Not all MySpace customisations are designed to make the pages flashier. Once you delve into this world, you'll find all sorts of things you can do to transform MySpace into your space.

The key to being able to modify MySpace beyond the features available from the service itself is that MySpace makes it possible to embed computer code called "HTML" (HyperText Markup Language) directly into certain parts of a user profile. With this code, users can do almost anything any Web designer could do, including change the background colours, add more pictures or videos, display animation, or link out to media or material on other websites.

HTML code looks a little like code from any programming language, and some tech-savvy MySpace users have taken the time to actually learn how to program in HTML, so that they can have a great deal of control over how their MySpace profile looks and works (**FIGURE 7.1**). But you don't really need to know anything about HTML to use it. That's because there are numerous websites that will automatically generate the code for you. All you have to do is copy it on to your Windows or Mac clipboard, point to the appropriate spot on your MySpace profile, and paste it in. Still, a little HTML knowledge goes a long way and will allow you to get the most out of the experience. We think that's a good thing, because it encourages teenagers to study HTML, which teaches them about Web design and computer programming, two skills that can be very useful for their futures.

```
<form action='http://www.kwiz.biz/simplesurveys/do-
survey.php' method='post' target='_new'><table border=1
bordercolor=#efefef cellspacing=0><tr><td valign=top
align=center colspan=2><b><i>TELL ME ABOUT YOURSELF - The
Survey</i></b><input type='hidden' name='question1'
value='TELL+ME+ABOUT+YOURSELF+-+The+Survey'><input
type='hidden' name='type1' value='2'></td
></tr><tr><td valign=top
```

FIGURE 7.1 Some (not all) HTML code is pretty hard to decipher, but it's definitely not rocket science, and there are lots of websites that will generate it for you.

Before You Customise

There are a couple of downsides to the ability to customise MySpace.

First, while a few choice profile customisations can make a profile more personal and cool, too much stuff can look cluttered or gaudy, or make it difficult for others to navigate your page. They could even keep a profile from functioning at all.

Second, poorly constructed custom MySpace profiles can freeze up your Web browser because of improper coding or excessive design elements. This is especially true when high-bandwidth items such as Flash animations, videos, and music are added.

Third, customisation can sometimes bring up some safety and computer-security issues. For example, some MySpacers like to fill out third-party surveys and post the results on their page, as we mentioned in Chapter 5. Some of these surveys encourage people to answer questions like "Have you been on drugs?" or "Have you stolen anything?" or "Have you ever been drunk?" Some even ask questions of a sexual nature. The third-party sites that host the surveys often generate HTML code, based on the answers the children provide, which MySpace users can use to post the survey results on their profiles. The downside to this technique, besides the fact that they are posting information about themselves that's better kept private, is that when you add code from an untrusted source to a MySpace profile, you run the risk of linking out to dangerous sites that could cause security or other problems for you or your computer and for people who visit your MySpace page (**FIGURE 7.2**).

```
In the past month have you gone Skinny
                          Dipping: nope
   In the past month have you Stolen
                        Anything: nope
                   Ever been Drunk: yeah
           Ever been called a Tease: yeah
              Ever been Beaten up: nope
                  Ever Shoplifted: nope
           How do you want to Die: by fire or in my sleep
What do you want to be when you Grow Up: ??????i donno yet
   What country would you most like to Visit: france
```

FIGURE 7.2 A portion of one of many third-party surveys available to MySpace users.

Keeping HTML From Doing Bad Things

The good news about HTML is that what goes in can also come out. Children who paste HTML on their profiles should look at the profile immediately to see if there are any problems. It's also a very good idea to check the profile on a regular basis to screen friends' comments, which can also contain HTML code along with text. If there are problems with code pasted into any of the fields in the Profile Edit section, you should go back to that section and remove the code, unless one of you happens to be an HTML wizard and can fix any errant code.

In addition to code that's pasted in the Profile Edit section, HTML can also be placed in photo captions, in descriptions for groups your child might moderate, and comments other people post in your child's profile. Teenagers need to be especially alert when it comes to code their friends include in comments. If there is a problem with that code or with any text in these sections, it can be edited using Safe Edit Mode (sometimes referred to as "Safe Mode").

To access Safe Edit Mode, follow these steps.

1. In the Hello box on your home page, click Edit Profile.

2. Click Safe Edit Mode near the upper right corner of the Profile Edit page (**FIGURE 7.3**).

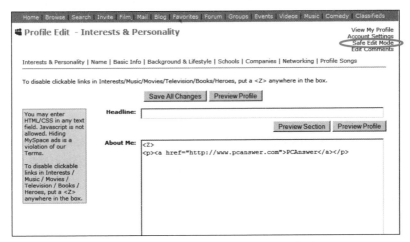

FIGURE 7.3 Click on Safe Edit Mode to remove HTML code from groups, comments, or photo captions.

3. Click Groups, Comments, or Images.

4. You can delete or edit code or text in Groups and Images. You can only delete code or text in comments (**FIGURE 7.4**).

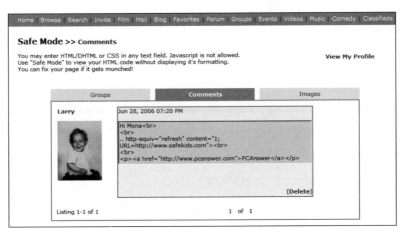

FIGURE 7.4 Safe Edit Mode lets you delete HTML code in groups, captions, and comments. Shown here is code that was entered as part of a comment by a friend.

Making Profiles Sing and Dance

It's very easy to add colour, graphics, and artistic personality to a MySpace profile by pasting HTML into the appropriate places. We'll explain how to do that in a minute, but first you need to know how to find or generate the code that you want to paste in. That's where MySpace Editors come in handy.

Using MySpace Editors

There are numerous sites on the Web that offer what are called "MySpace editors." They're easy-to-use interactive templates that generate HTML code based on information you provide so that you can jazz up your standard profile.

You don't need to know anything about HTML to use MySpace editors. For example, MySpace Editor (www.myspacecode.com) offers an easy-to-use online Profile Editor that lets you pick a different background colour, background image, and page border colour for your profile. You can preview how the new code will affect your page. When you're finished, you click the Generate Code button, and the website creates the HTML code, which you simply copy to the clipboard and paste in any of the fields in the Interests and Personality section of your profile (**FIGURE 7.5**).

FIGURE 7.5 One of the many sites that generate code for spiffing up profiles, mySpace Editor is free and easy to use.

Use Caution When Visiting Customisation Sites

Many of the sites that provide customisation codes make money through advertising, so it's not uncommon to get pop-ups and other obnoxious ads when you visit these sites. We can't vouch for the integrity of these sites, so if you visit them, use caution about providing any personal information. Keep in mind, too, that third-party sites like these tend to come and go, based on economics, as well as the legality of their business practices.

There are plenty of other online editors that you can use, including Thomas' MySpace Editor (http://206.225.92.10/myspace/) and, as you might expect, one called PimpMySpace (www.pimpmyspace.org) (**FIGURE 7.6**). You can find more in the link list at www.myspace-editors.com or by typing "MySpace editors" into any search engine.

PimpMySpace.Org

Everything you need to pimp out your profile!

1-312-685-7533 << Call for Help

Ads by Yahoo!

volleyball uniform
Huge selection of...
www.volleyballusa.com

Graphic Art Design
Find Deals on Graphic Art...
www.shopping.com

Welcome to PimpMySpace.org. The ultimate profile pimpin' solutions are available right here.

April 18th, 2006 - MySpace Avatars

FIGURE 7.6 PimpMySpace.org bills itself as the place for the "ultimate profile pimpin' solutions."

Pasting Code Into MySpace

You can paste the HTML code into several of the blank fields on the Profile Edit page. These fields are normally used by MySpace users to type in things like biogs, favourite movies, or people they would like to meet. But they can also be used to hold HTML code that will automatically be executed when people visit your profile. The fields in which the code can be placed include About Me, I'd Like to Meet, Interests, Music, Books, Movies, Television, and Heroes.

To place the code, do the following.

1. Copy the code from a MySpace editor or other source onto the clipboard.

2. From the Hello box of your MySpace home page, click Edit Profile.

3. Place your cursor into a field such as About Me or I'd Like to Meet and paste the code into the box. If there is already code or text in that field, you can add the code at the bottom (**FIGURE 7.7**).

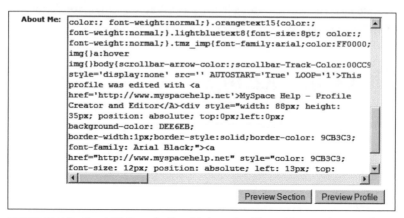

FIGURE 7.7 Pasting HTML code like this into the About Me or other text box of Profile Editor can change the look of your profile.

4. Click Preview Section to see what the HTML code does to your profile (**FIGURE 7.8**).

5. If you're happy with the change, scroll down to the bottom of the screen and click Save All Changes.

6. If you made a mistake or want to change anything, repeat the process to either remove or replace the code.

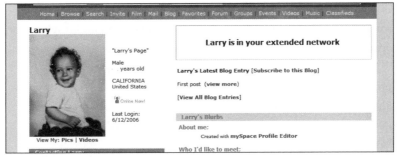

FIGURE 7.8 Larry's site with modified colours from mySpace Profile Editor. And, yes, that really is Larry!

Hotlinking

Hotlinking is a practice in which someone uses images or media files from another website by linking to them, rather than loading them on their own MySpace profile or using a hosting service (**FIGURE 7.9**). Because hotlinking is easier than uploading files to an appropriate server, MySpacers regularly use it, though it's not always legal. If the images or files that are being hotlinked are copyrighted and the borrower hasn't received authorisation to use them, hotlinking boils down to stealing.

```
<img src="picture.jpg" height="400" width="255">
```

FIGURE 7.9 One line of HTML code is all it takes to hotlink an image from someone else's site. Easy, but not always legal.

But that's not the only problem. Hotlinking also uses a lot of bandwidth, so the owner of the website hosting the files could potentially lose visitors if the site seems too slow because of the drain that hotlinking causes.

Another downside is that hotlinking can backfire because you have no control over the source location. If the other site goes down or is running slowly, your image won't show up. And if the webmaster of that other site changes or removes the image at any time, it will affect the link to your MySpace profile and ultimately what shows up.

To counteract rampant hotlinking that infringes on their bandwidth and intellectual property, mischievous webmasters have been known to replace original hotlinked images with others (advertisements, junk, or random posts) to discourage people from stealing their images. A malicious webmaster might even do worse and put a totally inappropriate or potentially embarrassing picture or comment in its place.

Because some MySpace users were in the process of linking out to photos and other media that violated the site's Terms of Use (pornographic images, for example), MySpace had to staff up. "We are now [as of spring 2006] reviewing every single image hotlinked to our site," a MySpace customer care staffer told us.

While conducting research for this book, we came across a discussion in a graphic artists' forum about MySpace, hotlinking, and artists' concerns about intellectual property. One artist admitted to renaming linked files so that they don't appear on MySpace users' pages any more and, in its place, creating a new file with the old name that says, "This [expletive deleted] is hotlinking a file without permission."

Linking Out From MySpace

Linking out from MySpace is different from hotlinking, and in most cases it's OK. Linking involves placing a link on a Web page—in this case a MySpace profile—that takes visitors to another website.

As a courtesy, it's a good idea to seek permission from the site that's being linked to. But sometimes, if it's a large site, it's not practical. With very few exceptions, linking is both legal and ethical. Links are created by embedding a small amount of HTML code in a MySpace profile that will allow visitors to go to that other site.

For example, if you wanted to place a link to our site, BlogSafety.com, within your profile, you would paste the following code in your About Me or other section, and that would be OK with us:
<a href="http://www.blogsafety.com">Visit BlogSafety.com</a>

Changing Top 8 Friends to Top 20

In Chapter 4 we discussed Your Top 8, the feature that lets MySpace users select eight people from their list of friends and then display them (in a certain order) on their profiles. This feature is currently the default, and no more than eight friends will appear in that space unless the user programs the page otherwise. Because the Top 8 in a way signifies a person's favourite friends, it can become a sensitive issue, since the list appears publicly on a Myspacer's profile.

Some advanced MySpace users try to avoid offending anyone by hacking their own profile to feature their Top 20 or Top 30 instead, or even to hide this section completely. One way to expand the Top 8 list is to visit MySpaceSupport.com and select Top 16 Friends List, which lets users display up to 40 top friends on their pages (**FIGURE 7.10**).

FIGURE 7.10 This form at MySpaceSupport.com makes it easy to modify a Top 8 list. If this were an active profile, you'd see real pictures, not placeholders.

Monitoring Visitors to Your Profile

There are numerous websites that offer tools that let you track who is visiting your page. Using a snippet of code that you post on your MySpace page, these sites track and record the MySpace users who are looking at your profile. You can find details like who, when, and what time of day they visited. Advanced spying code will even give you a link to their profiles and let you track the number of users who look at your profile over a period of a day, week, or month.

These Web tracking services are great for MySpace users who think they might have a stalker and want to monitor activity on their pages. It can also be useful for concerned parents who want to keep better tabs on who is visiting their children's pages (assuming they agree to post this on the page).

There's even a blog—myspacetracker.blogspot.com—that helps you keep track of all the different profile trackers (**FIGURE 7.11**).

FIGURE 7.11 A profile tracker from MySpaceReviews.com makes it easy to figure out who's been knocking on your virtual door or lurking on your profile.

Bots: Making Friends by the Thousands

In addition to being a place for friends, MySpace has also become a marketing and publicity tool. People and businesses use the site to promote their goods and services, and as MySpace continues to grow and build members, more people are making money (and even careers) out of MySpace promotion.

Automatic tools called "bots" are a big help for MySpace promoters (and often a big nuisance to everyone else) who want to target more users and extend their MySpace reach. A bot is a piece of software that interacts with Web pages—kind of like a person might, but it does it automatically. There are even companies that will mass-target MySpace users with friend requests, invitations, and more.

Bots are also used by some MySpace users to quickly build their friend base. Popular and cheap (even free) downloads for friend-generating bots are becoming more and more common. Nicknamed "Whore Trains" (ouch) or "Friend Trains," these tools help users send out massive friend requests with minimal effort (**FIGURE 7.12**).

AdderRobot

Adder Robot; hands down the #1 MySpace automation software to date.
Everything you need, without breaking your budget.

What is this?
Adder Robot is a MySpace automation program. Allowing you to let people know who you are.
Auto friend request, comment, message, group/event invite, bulletins etc...
This program is only permitted for MySpace's acceptable use; personal, band and film profiles.
Your audience can be found on **MySpace.com**

Try it before you buy it. Download a free demo version today:

Download

All registered users will have access to free updates.
Free updates and support, we dont forget about you.

FIGURE 7.12 A Web promotion for one of the many "bots" that can automate friend requests, etc.

Why would MySpace users want to spam a bunch of users with friend requests in hopes of adding more "friends" to their profile? Status. Publicity. Celebrity. And all those other things we talked about in Chapter 2. The My Friends space is in many ways a popularity contest, and—for some teenagers—the more "friends" they have, the "cooler" they are. Plus, users who've managed to build thousands of "friends" have a built-in network to advertise and promote whatever they might have going on in their lives, like music, writing, a small business, or events. MySpace is cheap advertising and an easy platform for up-and-coming somebodies from all walks of life to self promote.

Uploading Video

In Chapter 4, we wrote a bit about adding video to your profile. There are actually two ways to do that. You can use video that's already on MySpace (music videos from bands, for example) or you can upload your own video.

To search for and display on your MySpace profile a video that's already on MySpace, take the following steps.

1. On the blue navigation bar on any MySpace page, click Videos.

2. If you know what you're looking for, enter a search term in the text box and click Search Videos. Otherwise, browse through Top Videos or drill down into the categories via the Browse Categories tab (**FIGURE 7.13**).

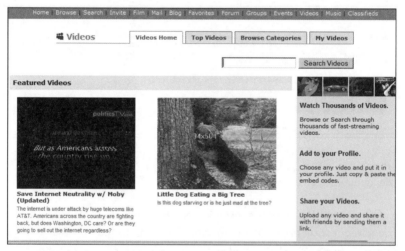

FIGURE 7.13 Searching for video.

3. When you've found a potential video, click the blue video title to view it (**FIGURE 7.14**). A media player should automatically load. (Once in a while, a computer glitch will cause media files not to play properly. If that happens, find the nearest computer expert— probably the nearest child in your house).

4. Click the Play key on the media player to view the video.

FIGURE 7.14 Select a video to display by clicking its title.

5. If you like what you see and want to include this clip on your profile, copy the code from the Video Code box on the right side of the screen.

6. Go to your MySpace home page, click Edit Profile, and paste the code into the About Me section. Then click Save All Changes. The video displays on your profile page.

To upload your own videos to the MySpace Video section, do this.

1. On the blue navigational bar at the top of any MySpace page, click Videos.

2. Click the My Videos tab at the top of the screen, and then click Upload Video (**FIGURE 7.15**).

FIGURE 7.15 Click the "Upload Video" button to transfer video from your hard drive.

3. On the Upload Video: Step 1 page, enter a short title and description (**FIGURE 7.16**).

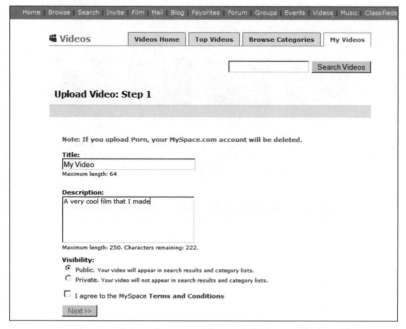

FIGURE 7.16 Name and describe your video and designate if it's public or private.

4. On the Upload Video: Step 2 page, select the appropriate categories your video falls into. You can also add tags (keywords) to help people find your video.

5. On the Upload Video: Step 3 page, browse your hard drive for the video and click Upload. Video files are generally quite large, so it may take a few minutes for the process to finish.

    The video must go through MySpace approval before it appears on your profile. Photos, on the other hand, are posted automatically but reviewed by MySpace after the fact, and can be reported by other users if they're in violation of the Terms of Use.

Children (and adults too) need to remember to consider their own privacy and the privacy of others when uploading videos (as well as photos, of course). For example, who's on display in a party video or family movie you want to upload? Have you asked their permission to be shown in a public "place"? MySpace has rules about what can and cannot be posted, including videos that contain nudity or violence or violate someone's copyright. Remind your children that their videos could be copied and passed around long into the future.

Forums for Learning About Customising

Another way to learn more about customising MySpace is to use the MySpace forums, where experts offer free advice to anyone who cares to visit. As we discussed in Chapter 4, a forum is an Internet venue specifically for holding discussions (in text) and are great resources for questions, help, and advice. MySpace has a forum dedicated to all things MySpace, with both a General topic and one that focuses just on customising. There are experts on these forums who will answer your questions. This is a great resource for finding code and learning how to do things with your profile

To browse MySpace forums, follow these steps.

1. Click on Forum via the blue navigational bar at the top of any MySpace screen.

2. On the Forum homepage, you'll see folders or categories with short descriptions about the forum.

3. Click on the MySpace topic and then go to either the Customising or General subtopic. Scroll through the posts until you see one that has something interesting or addresses what you are looking for (**FIGURE 7.17**).

FIGURE 7.17 An active MySpace customising forum where experts share their experiences.

To post a topic, do the following.

1. Click Post a Topic.

2. Enter a subject and type your question or discussion, and click Post This Topic.

3. You'll see a Preview Topic confirmation screen. Click Post This Topic to publish your comment (**FIGURE 7.18**).

FIGURE 7.18 Posting a question on the MySpace message forum.

Now you know some of the most popular customisation options that ambitious profile designers use—way more than any busy parent would want to take on. But you can at least talk intelligently about profile design with just about any teenage MySpace user. And if you've created your own profile and tried out even a few of our suggestions, you're way ahead of the average parent—of most people over 30, in fact!

It's time to step away from the computer and back into your role as both a good parent and a concerned citizen. After explaining how teenagers use MySpace and other social networks and how you can use it and help them make the experience safer, we're ready for the final and, ultimately, the most challenging chapter. Where do we as parents and a society go from here to make public policy that keeps pace with and encourages children's constructive use of Web 2.0?

CHAPTER 8

Where Do We Go From Here?

A BOOK ABOUT SOCIAL networking is like suspended animation: remember those old cartoons in which Wile E. Coyote and the Road Runner would suddenly be suspended mid-air, right at the most dramatic moment of the fastest action of the entire episode, the Coyote within millimetres of (and yet so very far from) the ultimate attainment? Of course, in the case of this book, the ultimate attainment is enough public understanding of MySpace and social networking to allow for just the right balance of free expression and safety.

Our challenge is that not only are MySpace, social networking, and the Web moving targets, but so is public awareness. By its very nature the user-driven Web is unpredictable. It's a *collective* product, process, experience, and experiment. So all of us are determining where the Web is headed, and ideally we're safety-trained, critically thinking participants. But despite this inherent unpredictability, there are some things we're pretty sure about from close observation since the early days of the Web.

Teenagers Are in the Driver's Seat

Web 2.0 is not going away any time soon, and it's hardly something we can control (except perhaps in our own homes). In fact, the interactive, user-produced Web is growing astonishingly fast, according to figures from communications regulator Ofcom. Their most recent report on the UK communications market says that while 40 per cent of adults with Internet access have used social-networking sites such as MySpace, Friends Reunited and Bebo and that figure rises to 70 per cent among 16–24-year-olds, and over half of them use the sites at least weekly.

So the socialising or creative networking part of Web 2.0 is not only here to stay, but increasingly what the Web is all about. The Web is not just a teenagers' hangout, but also their storage locker, research tool, communications tool, entertainment medium, and news channel—and the distinctions between these functions are increasingly blurred.

However, here's what we *do* know.

- **Internet natives.** Our children are the "digital natives," or those who have not known life without the Internet. And we "digital immigrants" need to interact—to learn *as* we teach media literacy and online safety—so we can effectively parent our Net-fluent children.

- **Influence v. control.** The more we try to control a user-driven medium like Web 2.0, the more workarounds its producers find—whether we're talking about laws or parenting. In this media environment, it's the responsible websites and obedient children who are reached by the rules, not the irresponsible or defiant ones. Some fresh thinking, parenting, and governing are needed if we want to influence the latter.

- **A blurred distinction.** More and more of our childrens' lives are either online or mirrored online, as the distinction between online and offline continues to fade in their minds.

- **A healthy scepticism.** The need for critical thinking about whom we're interacting with and what we're consuming and expressing is only growing—for all of us—because so much is done in public and can be recorded forever.

- **Identity play.** Wherever anonymity is allowed—wherever identity can't be confirmed—teenagers will play with identity by trying on different personas, which is usually, but not always, constructive.

- **Support risk asssessment.** Teenagers experiment and take risks in the process of learning who they are socially, emotionally, and physically, and we do them a disservice if we don't let them or if we try to remove all risk.

- **Uploading too.** On Web 2.0, parents need to be concerned not only with inappropriate material that children "download," but personal information and material that they "upload."

- **Perspective needed.** We need to put risks into context. While there are dangers in social networking, children face a far greater danger from people they already know. Do we ban school, religious and family gatherings because of the risk of predators in those venues, or do we teach children critical thinking skills that can protect them online and offline?

- **Life literacy/computer literacy.** Remember "Parental guidance suggested." Transfer all that good parenting sense you already have into cyberspace. Don't worry if you don't have your childrens' level of computer literacy—they can help you with that. They need your guidance on life literacy.

- **Interactive solution development.** It's OK that parents don't have all the answers. Schools, politicans, and police don't either. Nor do we, of course. Not having all the answers forces us all to talk about social networking—in our homes, schools, and communities. This interdependence is a good thing because on a user-driven, social Web, the solutions need to be collective, interactive, and evolving too.

Parents in the Car

Just as young drivers in training need an experienced driver in the car, parents need to be "in the car" where teenagers' online social lives are concerned. In the same way that we ask them, "Who are you going out with tonight?" or "Who else is going to the gig or party?" we also need to ask them who they're spending time with online.

Remember that it doesn't help a learner driver to have someone in the car who is petrified by teenage fatality statistics and has buried the keys in the garden. It just helps to have someone in the passenger seat, offering guidance and pointers along the way.

There Ought to Be a Law. . .

Just before we put this book to bed, we took a couple of days to help moderate a one-day conference on social-networking safety sponsored by the US National Center for Missing & Exploited Children. Panellists included law enforcement leaders, leading paediatricians, online safety experts, the Attorneys General of Connecticut and North Carolina, the CEO of Xanga, the Chief Privacy Officer of Facebook and, for his first public appearance since taking the job, Hemanshu Nigam, the chief security officer for Fox Interactive, the parent company of MySpace.

The day saw some lively and sometimes contentious discussions. One safety expert advised parents not to let those under 17 use services like MySpace except under close parental supervision. The politicians called upon the industry to voluntarily restrict access to only those who are over 16 and to enforce that by using age verification. All this despite the fact that John Cardillo, CEO of Sentry, a leading provider of identity, background and age verification, explained that while verifying the age of adults might be practical, it is impossible to verify the ages of people under 17 because there are no publicly available records that can be used to confirm their identities in the US or Europe.

We also heard from John Draper and Christopher Le of the US National Suicide Prevention Lifeline who said that referrals from MySpace users have become the largest source of calls to the hotline. Increasingly, children are using their profiles "to in some ways convey that they had suicidal intent," said Draper in a followup interview. "There is very much the potential for saving lives because the first people to hear about kids at risk are other kids." The government-funded organisation is setting up suicide prevention profiles on MySpace, Xanga and Facebook. We don't know how many lives can be saved as a result of referrals through social networks, but it's certainly something that should be thought about by policy makers seeking to restrict young people's access to these sites. This is just one powerful example of how monitoring teenagers' social networking can be much more beneficial to young people than banning it.

The politicians who spoke at the meeting we attended are not the only elected officials calling for government regulation of social networking. In the UK there are no plans for MySpace-specific legislation and in fact the word "MySpace" doesn't appear even once in *Hansard*, the record of what is said in Parliament. However in the United States the Deleting Online Predators Act 2006 would restrict the use of social-networking sites from school and library computers, as if that were actually where the danger lies.

It is easy to understand why politicians would want to regulate MySpace and similar companies. After all the scary news stories, regulation might seem like a way to protect children from "unlawful sexual advances, unlawful requests for sexual favours, or repeated offensive comments of a sexual nature from adults," as the Deleting Online Predators act phrases it. While these elected officials are certainly well-meaning, if we've learned anything from our research for this book, it's that banning social networks not only won't make children safer, it will actually put them at greater risk.

We understand public officials' concerns and applaud them for thinking about our children's safety, but we also urge them to fund research and carefully study the issues before passing laws or asking the courts to intervene. To us, it seems too early to pass a law concerning social networking. There's too much we don't know and much research to be done, which makes legislation at this point seem reactive and uninformed.

Susan's Story

Let's end with a story that illustrates the extent to which teenagers are continually evolving and why open communication between them and us is a good thing.

"Susan" (not her real name) is an avid MySpace user (her real age is 14). Her parents, who are friends of Larry's, called us because they were concerned Susan was posting too much private information on MySpace, and they didn't understand "this social-networking thing." At the time, she was displaying her full name, lots of pictures of herself, where she went to school, where she hung out after school, and information and pictures from many of her friends. She lied about her age, saying she was over 16 so that she could post a public profile.

Larry had a heart-to-heart chat with Susan, explaining that she really needed to take some steps to protect her privacy. It wasn't a lecture—no scare tactics were used—just an honest discussion of the risks.

We also enlisted Susan's help as we wrote this book and created our website, asking her to help us better understand the way teenagers are using MySpace. Larry and Susan talked for quite a while, with Larry asking most of the questions. It wasn't one of those patronising conversations where the adult asks questions as a *show* of interest. It was genuine interest because we needed Susan's expertise. She added Larry to her friends list as part of his MySpace training, a very generous act on her part.

During those conversations, something unexpected happened. Susan, who is very reluctant to discuss social networking with her parents or other adults, not only opened up and told us a great deal, but she started to listen as well. The next thing we knew, she had withdrawn some of her personal information, including her last name, posted new photos that were a bit less provocative, and used her real age, which meant that her profile became private.

But then something else happened. The next time we checked in on her profile, she'd changed her display name to include a sexually suggestive four-letter word, and there was more sexually suggestive material on her page. This was a little tough for Larry—while he isn't her parent, he felt he and Susan had made some great progress.

So they had another chat. She told him her profile's new look was all an "inside joke" between her and her friends. He pointed out that, even though her profile was private, her very provocative display name was public and that it might be possible for some of the material on her page to find its way to the wrong people. Susan didn't respond, but she apparently listened *again* because, within a few weeks, she'd changed her disturbing display name and removed some of the age-inappropriate material.

Of course, there's nothing to stop Susan from taking unnecessary risks once again. She, like MySpace and our understanding of social networking, is a work in progress. Fourteen-year-olds, like websites, are subject to change without notice. Before we know it, she'll likely be driving a car, going out on real (not just virtual) dates, going to parties where others are perhaps drinking or using drugs, and taking all sorts of other risks. Neither we nor her parents will always be in that car, and we certainly won't be at the parties or along on dates. We can influence her behaviour, but we can't control it. And it's important that we not overreact, so that we can continue to have some influence on her decision making.

By far her most effective safeguard, though, is Susan's growing proficiency in fine-tuning a filter that works infinitely better than anything we or her parents could possibly install on her PC. This filter is the software running on the computer between her ears—her own developing critical thinking skills and her ability to make appropriate decisions. Susan doesn't know it, but her experience on MySpace and the adults around her who are listening and gently guiding her are helping her get rid of some of the bugs in that software. Susan's going to be just fine.

You may disagree—and if you do, we hope you'll come talk with us about it. See you online at www.BlogSafety.com!

Index

A

About Me section, 37
account settings, 48–52
  away message, 52
  block user setting, 49
  music settings, 51–52
  profile settings, 49–50
account setup, 28–34
  home page, 32–34
  inviting friends, 31–32
  photo uploads, 30–31
  signup process, 28–29
accounts
  cancelling, 61–63, 147–148
  deleting, 147
  setting up, 28–34
Add to Friends link, 68
Add/Edit Photos link, 54
address book, 74–75
adolescents. *See* teenagers
avatars, 5
away message, 52

B

background information, 39–40
bands
  adding profile songs from,
    56–57, 58
  blocking friend requests from, 46
  disabling songs from, 47
Bebo, 8, 11
Berry, Justin, 117
birthday display option, 46
Blocked Users feature, 49
blocking
  bulletins, 76
  users, 49
Blog Safe mode, 104
blogs, 2, 6, 102–104

  comments on, 104
  privacy options, 46, 103–104
  Safe mode, 104
  safety tips for, 133
  setting up, 102–103
BlogSafety.com, 23, 24, 99, 132, 133,
  134, 138
books
  community related to, 89–90
  specifying interests in, 37
bots, 162–163
Boyd, Danah, 15, 15, 18, 20, 22, 24
Boys & Girls Clubs of America, 132
bulletins, 75–76
  blocking, 76
  posting, 75
  reading, 76, 77
bullying, 115, 119–120

C

calendars, 60–61
cancelling accounts, 61–63, 147–148
captions, 55
Cardillo, John, 174
chat rooms, 95–98
  logging on to, 95–96
  parenting points on, 96, 98
Child Exploitation and Online
  Protection (CEOP) Centre, 10, 137
child pornography, 128–129
children
  cancelling account of, 147
  filtering content for, 146–147
  finding online, 139–142
  monitoring online, 144–146
  parental input for, 132
  safe blogging tips for, 133
children go online, 113, 115
classmates, finding, 92–93, 141, 142

Comedy community, 90–91
comments, 78–83
   approving, 45, 81
   blog, 104
   deleting, 82–83
   picture, 80
   privacy, 81
   profile, 79
communities, 6–7, 20–22, 86–99
   Books, 89–90
   chat rooms, 95–98
   Comedy, 90–91
   Film, 89
   finding, 87
   forums, 98–99
   Games, 91
   Music, 87–89
   Schools, 91–95
Companies link, 41
Connect.ee, 11
Contact MySpace link, 135–136
Contacting box, 68
Cooper, Jeff, 146
Cooper, Sharon, 115
Costi, Lee, 112
creative networking, 3–5
Crimes Against Children Research
   Centre, 112, 113
critical thinking, 173
customising profiles, 53–59, 153–161
   caution about sites for, 157
   changing Top 8 list, 160–161
   downsides to, 153–154
   forums for learning about, 167–169
   MySpace editors for, 156–157
   pasting HTML code for, 157–158
   phrases related to, 152
   Safe Edit mode and, 154–155
cyberbullying, 115, 119–120
Cyberspace Research Unit, 113
Cyworld.com, 11

D

Daily Mail, 24, 111
Dannahey, Frank, 109, 113, 114
decorating spaces, 5–6

deleting
   accounts, 148
   blog comments, 104
   comments, 82–83
   friends, 78
Deleting Online Predators Act, 175
designing spaces, 5–6
digital natives, 172
display name, 38–39
Draper, John, 174

E

Edit Profile link, 36
editing profiles, 156–157
Eichewald, Kurt, 117
email
   account cancellation and, 147–148
   MySpace mail feature, 71–74
   parenting point on, 74
eSPINtheBottle.com, 19
events, 83–84
exposure, 22

F

Facebook, 9, 94–95
Federal Bureau of Investigation
   (FBI), 11
Film community, 89
filtering software, 146–147
finding
   classmates, 92–93, 141, 142
   communities, 87
   your child online, 139–142
forums, 98–99
   BlogSafety, 99, 138
   browsing, 167
   MySpace customising, 167–169
   parenting point on, 99
   participating in, 98–99
   posting topics to, 168
   school, 93–94
friends, 66–70
   accepting friend requests, 69–70
   adding to friends list, 66–68
   deleting from friends list, 78

friend *continued*
    denying friend requests, 69–70
    inviting, 31–32, 67–68
    parenting point on, 70
    privileges of, 66
Friendster, 2, 3

G

Gamble, Jim, 16
Games community, 91
Grouper.com, 59
groups
    invitations to, 46
    music, 88
    school, 93–94

H

hacking, 152
harrassment, 119
headline, 37
Hello page, 32–34
heroes, 37
Hi5.com, 11
Hide Online Now option, 46
home page, 32–34
hotlinking, 159–160
HotorNot.com, 86
HTML, 49–51, 152–153
    customising profiles with, 156–160
    hotlinking with, 159–160
    parenting point on using, 51
    pasting code into MySpace,
        157–158
    Safe Edit Mode and, 154–155
HTML Comments option, 50
Huffaker, David, 16

I

IamBigBrother software, 146
identity play, 173
Imbee.com, 143
impersonators, 148
inappropriate content, 128–129, 135

influence v. control, 172
informal learning, 16
instant messaging, 100–102
interest communities, 6
interests
    networking, 41–42
    personal, 36–38
Interests & Personality page, 35–38
Internet Archive, 124–128
Internet Watch Foundation, 129, 137
invitations
    event, 83–84
    friend, 31–32, 67–68
    group, 46

J

journals, 6

K

Koch, Wendy, 110

L

Le, Christopher, 174
Leary, Mary, 129
legal risks, 127–128
life literacy, 173
lifestyle information, 39–40
Li, Kenneth, 4
links
    hotlinking, 159–160
    linking out, 160
logging in/out, 34
Lunarstorm.se, 11
lurkers, 97

M

mail feature, 71–74
    parenting point on, 74
    reading messages, 72
    sending messages, 72–73
Manage Calendar link, 60
misconduct, reporting, 54, 135–138
Mobile Settings, 49

monitoring
    services for, 144–145
    software for, 145–146
    visitors, 161–162
movies
    community related to, 89
    specifying interests in, 37
multisocialising, 19–20
music
    adding to profiles, 56–57, 58
    community related to, 87–89
    specifying interests in, 37
music settings, 51–52
MySpace, 3–5
    account settings, 48–52
    address book, 74–75
    blogs, 102–104
    bulletins, 75–76
    calendars, 60–61
    cancelling accounts, 61–63,
        147–148
    comments, 78–83
    communities, 86–99
    contacting, 135–138
    customising, 53–59, 153–161,
        167–169
    events, 83–84
    instant messaging, 100–102
    mail feature, 71–74
    page appearance differences, 71
    photo ratings, 84–86
    privacy settings, 43–48
    profiles, 34–48
    setup process, 28–34
MySpace editors, 156–157
MySpace FAQ, 136
MySpaceIM, 100–102
MySpaceReviews.com, 162
MySpaceSupport.com, 161
MySpaceWatch.com, 144, 145
myYearbook.com, 9, 10

N
Name page, 38–39
National Center for Missing &
    Exploited Children (NCMEC),
    129, 174

networking interests, 41–42
New Friend Requests! message, 69
nicknames, 39
Nigam, Hemanshu, 174
nude photos, 54, 128

O
online communities, 2
online selves, 14
Orkut.com, 11
overexposure, 24

P
parental controls, 143–147
parents
    importance of input from, 132
    online search for children by,
        139–142
    social-networking tips for, 134
passwords, 125
personality details, 36–38
perspective, 173
phishing schemes, 124–126
Photobucket.com, 54
photos, 53–56
    adding captions to, 55
    comments about, 80
    no forwarding option, 46
    parenting points on, 54, 56
    prohibitions on, 54, 128
    rating system for, 84–86
    uploading to profiles, 30–31,
        54–55
picture comments, 80
pimping, 152
PimpMySpace, 157
pornography, 128–129
posting
    blog comments, 104
    bulletins, 75
    topics to forums, 168
predators, sexual. *See* sexual predators
privacy
    blogs and, 103–104
    commenting and, 81
    downside of, 122

privacy *continued*
  instant messaging and, 101
  older teenagers and, 135
  online safety and, 121–122
  setting options for, 43–48
Profile Edit page
  Background & Lifestyle page,
    39–40
  Companies link, 41
  Interests & Personality page,
    35–38
  Name page, 38–39
  Networking page, 41–42
  Schools page, 40–41
  View My Profile link, 42
profile settings, 49–50
profile songs, 56–57, 58
profiles, 5, 7, 34–48
  background information, 39–40
  comments about, 79
  customising, 53, 156–161
  display name, 38–39
  editing, 156–157
  employer information, 41
  general interests, 36–38
  HTML code in, 152–153
  lifestyle information, 39–40
  monitoring visitors to, 161–162
  music added to, 56–57, 58
  networking interests, 41–42
  personality details, 36–38
  photos added to, 30–31, 54–55
  privacy settings, 43–48
  reviewing, 42
  school information, 40–41
  searching for, 139–141
  videos added to, 57, 59–60,
    164–167
  view options, 47
public journals, 6

Q

QQ.com, 11
questionnaires, 117–118

R

ranking photos, 84–86
RateMe.com, 86
reading
  bulletins, 76, 77
  mail messages, 72
removing. *See* deleting
Report Inappropriate Content link,
  135
Report This Image link, 54
reporting misconduct, 54, 135–138
Rifkin, Evan, 12
risk assessment, 24, 114–115, 173
Rivin, Adrien Survol, 118
romantic interests, 40
Roosevelt, Franklin D., 130

S

Safe Edit Mode, 154–155
safety issues, 107–130
  cyberbullying and, 115, 119–120
  guidelines related to, 132, 133–134
  inappropriate material and,
    128–129
  Internet Archive and, 123–124
  legal risks and, 127–128
  parenting points on, 113, 116, 122,
    125, 126, 129
  passwords and, 125–126
  phishing schemes and, 124–125
  pornography and, 128–129
  privacy and, 121–123
  research related to, 108–114
  risk assessment and, 114–129
  school policies and, 127
  security software and, 126
  sexual predation and, 108–114,
    115–117, 118–119
  surveys/questionnaires and, 118
safety tips, 30
school forums, 93–94
schools
  browsing MySpace by, 141, 142
  including in profiles, 40–41

schools *continued*
    Internet-use policies, 127
Schools community, 91–95
    finding classmates, 92–93
    locating school groups, 93–94
Search feature, 139–141
security software, 126
sending mail messages, 72–73
sexual orientation, 40
sexual predators
    parenting points on, 113, 116
    research about, 108–113
    scenarios related to, 115
    special risks related to, 118
    victim grooming methods,
        116–117
    See also safety issues
sharing calendars, 60–61
signing in/out, 34
signup process, 28–29
social networking, 2
software
    filtering, 146–147
    monitoring, 145–146
    security, 126
students
    Facebook site and, 9, 94–95
    finding, 92–93, 141, 142
suggestive photos, 56
suicide prevention, 174–175
surveys, 118

T
TagWorld.com, 12
tech literacy, 173
teenagers
    privacy options for, 135
    safe blogging tips for, 133
    sexual predators and, 109–110
    See also children
television interests, 37
terms of use agreement, 30
Toft, Richard, 119

Top 8 list, 76–77, 160–161
Top 16 Friends List, 161
topics, posting, 168
tracking
    services for, 161–162
    software for, 146
'tweens, 143

U
university students, 94–95
uploading
    photos, 30–31, 54–55
    profile songs, 56–57
    risks of, 173
    videos, 164–167
URLs (uniform resource locators), 33

V
videos
    adding to profiles, 57, 59–60,
        164–167
    parenting points on, 59–60, 167
    searching for and viewing, 164
    uploading, 164–167
View My Profile link, 42
Virtual Global Taskforce, 112
visitors, monitoring, 161–162
Vorderman, Carol, 112

W
Web 2.0, 172
Web logs. *See* blogs
Wikipedia, 9
Willard, Nancy, 120
Wolak, Janis, 113

X
Xanga, 174

Y
YouTube.com, 54, 59